P9-BYZ-932

COLIN COWIE'S
EXTRAORDINARY
WEDDINGS

FROM A GLIMMER OF AN IDEA TO A LEGENDARY EVENT

COLIN COWIE

CLARKSON POTTER/PUBLISHERS
NEW YORK

Copyright © 2006 by CAW Cowie, Inc., a California Corporation

All rights reserved.
Published in the United States by Clarkson Potter/Publishers,
an imprint of the Crown Publishing Group,
a division of Random House, Inc., New York.
www.crownpublishing.com
www.clarksonpotter.com

Clarkson N. Potter is a trademark and Potter and colophon
are registered trademarks of Random House, Inc.

Library of Congress Cataloging-in-Publication Data
Cowie, Colin, 1962–
Extraordinary weddings : from the glimmer of an idea
to a legendary event / Colin Cowie.—1st ed.
p.   cm.
1. Weddings—Planning.   I. Title.
HQ745.C675   2003
395.2'2–dc21   2002155159

ISBN: 978-1-4000-4872-4

Printed in China

10 9 8 7 6 5 4 3 2 1

First Edition

This book is dedicated to all the brides and grooms who have inspired me over the years. Many of them have become lifelong friends, and for some I'm honored to serve as godparent to their children. To every one of you: Thank you for enriching my life and for your everlasting friendship.

CONTENTS

INTRODUCTION

A wedding on a cliff-top in Capri . . . or on a white sandy beach in Paradise Island . . . or on the stage of the Metropolitan Opera . . . or amidst the beautiful vineyards of the Santa Ynez Valley . . . or in a lush hotel garden overlooking the Grand Canal in Venice . . . and I'm just getting warmed up. What's it like to plan a wedding on a grand scale? For me, weddings are pure, living, breathing theater, and holding one is akin to producing and directing a one-night-only all-star Broadway show. Using every sense at my disposal, I aim to tell an utterly transporting story, with a carefully thought-out beginning, middle, and end, a three-act spectacle that keeps guests delighted, thrilled, and—I hope—completely bedazzled.

But first things first. I'll start by sitting down with the bride and groom, armed with a list of questions that allow me to get at the essence of who they are and what they are envisioning. What would you like to communicate to your friends and family members about yourselves? Is there a story you'd like to convey? A memorable idea? From a thematic point of view, will your wedding suggest "1940s Hollywood glamour," "understated New England elegance," or "contemporary chic and sexy"? What about the setting? Do you envision a springtime ceremony under the cherry trees? A barefoot ceremony on a sunny beach? A January blowout in front of a roaring fire at a rustic ski lodge? Will you get married in your hometown or in some exotic locale? Will you invite four hundred guests or forty? Are you working with a tight budget, or can you reach, quite literally, for the stars? (An intimate wedding for forty people in your family's backyard demands the same amount of planning, scripting, pre-rehearsal, and attention to detail as does an extravaganza for twelve hundred guests— though, granted, on a much smaller scale!) Love is in the details, and no detail should be overlooked.

Next, I'll make note of my own ideas about the bride, the groom, their interests, their passions, and their personalities. Perhaps the bride loves ruby red. Perhaps the groom is a huge jazz aficionado. Perhaps they want to get married in a location that has meaning to them as a couple—the setting where he proposed, or where they shared a first kiss, a bottle of champagne, the realization that they'd found their soul mate. And so I'll get to work.

My inspirations begin with the smallest glimmer of an idea. I'll spy a swatch of emerald-green and gold silk brocade in a Mexican bazaar... glimpse a fabulous Schiaparelli pink ostrich feather in a museum...a lacy piece of coral in a souvenir shop...a flawless buttercup peeking out of a mossy old clay pot in somebody's yard...and my imagination goes into overdrive. It's my God-given gift to suddenly imagine the entire event in three acts, and three dimensions...four dimensions...why stop there? When I close my eyes, I can see, smell, taste, hear, and experience the whole nine yards from start to finish: the upholstered fabric walls, the framed picture windows, the spectrum of colors, the shape of the tables, the combination of flowers and containers, the lights, the music, the dance floor. I'll grab the nearest pencil and just start sketching, making copious notes as the images unfold. The trick is to keep from censoring my creative instincts—to simply let my eyes and hands and brain channel "fabulous"!

My ultimate ambition, always, is to make whichever wedding I'm putting together everything it can and should be. I push the envelope as far as possible. In every single one of the events I've been entrusted to orchestrate, I've woven the themes the bride, groom, and I came up with into each element of our celebration, from the menu, to our choice of music, to our tabletops, to our sinful and sublime desserts.

Again, as with all theatrical productions, I can't emphasize enough the importance of rehearsal. From start to finish, practice, practice, practice! Depending on the size and the scope of the wedding, a rehearsal could take place the night before, or it could involve a thorough run-through well in advance of the wedding weekend. In the latter case, this means sampling the food and wines at the table that's been designed. Is the crab cake too spicy? Are the chairs comfortable? How does the crystal feel in your hand? Are the linens the correct color? Can you see the person across from you, or is the centerpiece blocking him out? It means having a final fitting for the bride's gown, complete with hair, makeup, jewelry, and shoes. And it means taking time to rehearse everything, from the moment the flower girl scatters petals down the aisle, to where and how everyone exits after the "I dos" are completed. Of course, huge wedding parties require even more coordination and direction. With several bridesmaids and groomsmen, all admittedly a bit nervous, there's bound to be some confusion and stage fright: "When do I enter?" "How quickly or slowly do I walk down the aisle?" "Where do I stand when I reach the altar?" These are all questions that should be addressed during the rehearsal, which I'll typically schedule for the night before the wedding. But even a walk-through a few hours before the ceremony is fine—just so long as everyone is present and accounted for, including one or two musicians (to provide musical cues) and the officiant. I then line everyone up in order and take them right down the aisle, pointing out all the positioning, and making sure everyone understands the rhythm and flow of the procession and recession.

Of course, I can't help but give the bride a few crucial tips: That when she gets to the top of the aisle, she should silently count to five before taking her first steps (this provides an ideal photo opportunity). That she should keep her shoulders back, her head held high, and her bouquet as low as possible (that way, she appears confident, taller, and thinner—three things most of us aspire to be). That if her parents are escorting her down the aisle, they should walk a half-step behind her (to prevent them from accidentally stepping on her gown, or worse, tripping her), or that she might want to consider walking down half the aisle on her own and meeting her father, mother, or both halfway. Most of all, even if she's shaking in her heels, she must remember to take a deep breath and savor this moment, which has probably been in the works for the better part of a year, and in her dreams for the better part of a lifetime.

By the time the wedding day arrives, I've taken what was a glimmer of an idea and turned it into a sleek, well-oiled machine that's now running at breakaway speed. The cake is frosted. The band is tuning up. The wedding has become a full-scale production. It has a heartbeat, it has a soul, it has its own distinct energy. When my clients are happy, you can feel that joy in the air—and frankly, there's no greater feeling in the world.

Having said all this, if a bride or groom tells me they want, or expect, a "perfect" wedding, I tell them that they've come to the wrong man. I don't do "perfect" weddings. I don't do perfect anything. Perfection is a setup for a potential fall. Take my word for it: Something can always go wrong. The musicians might arrive late, the specially ordered vintage of wine doesn't arrive at all, the cognac roses look suspiciously like apricot roses, the bride has a skirmish with her mother, the wedding cake falls over (after twenty years of planning weddings, I could write a book on this subject alone). That's life. Nature happens. But I also make the solemn promise that (a) I will be your closest friend, your arbiter of taste, your trusted shrink, (b) I will do my absolute best for you, and (c) either I or a member of my team will handle whatever problem comes up, with the least impact on the bride and groom, or on their guests. The kitchen might be on fire, but I'll walk through the room calmly as if nothing is wrong. Forget the Oscars; I've taken home the "coolest cucumber on the planet" prize more times than I care to count. For readers who don't have the benefit of a wedding planner, remember that the reason people get married has nothing to do with impressing anyone. It has to do with surrounding yourself with family members and great friends who are there to witness and celebrate the most important day of your life. An off-color flower arrangement or a broken wineglass cannot take away from the spirit of the festivities. Chasing after perfection is not the point here!

So, why do I take such delight in my job? It's that exhilarating moment just before I cue the musicians for a ceremony. It's seeing a huge crowd of smiling faces bathed in the glow of candlelight, everybody dressed to the nines, and knowing that my creativity and effort has paid off. It's being able to work with the most extraordinary ingredients, canvases, hotels, flowers, wines—and most of all, with the most fantastically dedicated team of people imaginable, people whom I have grown to love and respect. I'm proud to say that my crew members are all graduates of the University of Whatever It Takes. We have traveled the world, laughed uncontrollably, spent countless hours finding the right solution, and come together in times of crisis. We all have our Ph.D.s in pushing the envelope and going that extra mile. If guests have their pictures taken with the bride and groom at the wedding reception, rest assured that the photograph will be developed, framed in silver, and waiting on their bedside table when they arrive back at their hotel at the end of the evening. Voilà!

And yet I never wait for the end of the evening to leave one of my productions. I usually depart following the cake cutting or when most of the guests begin saying their good-byes. Believe me when I say it's not because I get tired or bored—far from it. It's because I want my lasting memory of the night to be glamorous, joyous, celebratory, and sexy; a fantasy-image of sheer heaven that will remain in my mind's eye forever. It pains me to watch our crew perched on ladders, ripping swags of filmy silk off the ceilings, tossing linens into a laundry truck, removing a carefully constructed fountain that my incredible team spent weeks assembling. In theatrical terms, I don't like to see the stage get struck. I suppose I'm a hopeless romantic, but there are worse things to be.

The weddings you are about to visit were both a blessing and an enormous privilege to plan and be a part of, from the original inspiration all the way through to the final grand-scale production. If I may say so, they are all tributes to planning, artistry, imagination, detail, and round-the-clock teamwork. And I'll be the luckiest man on earth if they are remembered by everyone who was there as a tribute to love. Here's hoping that the weddings in this book will inspire readers, and remind them of possibilities of romance and joy they might not have dreamed of. The examples may be lavish, but readers will surely find ideas here that they can incorporate into their own celebrations—not to mention a bucket-load of great advice, from picking the right vows, to choosing the right makeup and wedding gown, to creating a memorable destination wedding.

Here's to believing that we all deserve the fairy tale, and that your wedding can be the first taste of Happily Ever After.

A THOUSAND ACRES

Jodi Barrack and Sean Pitts

SANTA YNEZ, CALIFORNIA

JUNE 30, 2001

As I swooped and circled over the Barrack ranch on a helicopter reconnaissance mission, it became obvious why bride Jodi Barrack had her heart set on getting married at home, in the Santa Ynez Valley, an hour north of Santa Barbara, California. The Barrack ranch was truly spectacular: a thousand halcyon acres of rolling hills, sumptuous vineyards, paddocks, and pastures, a perfectly restored manor house, and four lime-hued polo fields that came together to create the most expansive lawn I'd ever seen.

The right setting wasn't the only important thing to Jodi. Family, heritage, tradition, and pure kick-up-your-heels fun also counted. Her paternal grandparents are Lebanese. The bride and her fiancé, Sean Pitts, both love Hawaii, where they lived together for a year after college. Then there was the wine factor. Jodi's father, Tom, a real-estate developer and investor, bought the Santa Barbara property a decade earlier and planted vineyards whose first harvest was due around the same time Jodi and Sean were to wed. As for the kick-up-your-heels part? Jodi and Sean agreed that the wedding, and the after-party, should be such a blast that their guests would still be dancing when the sun rose.

The Middle East. Hawaii. Wine. The Santa Ynez mountains. Any single one of these motifs could have set the stage for a fantastic, over-the-top celebration, but as far as I was concerned, the more the merrier. We would create an exotic, wine-tinged Moroccan celebration, with elements of rustic California and airy Hawaii thrown into the mix.

All three of us leapt at the idea of having grapes as a motif on the wedding invitation and collateral. Using distinctive fuchsia ink on a thick, tactile cotton-rag board, we branded each invitation with a gold-embossed cluster of grapes, then wrapped each card in decorative Cabernet-colored Japanese paper and, finally, a hand-dyed silk ribbon.

We wound our wine motif and its various hues—passionate rubies, purples, burgundies, and Bordeaux—around whatever we could, from the flowers to the bridesmaids' Nicole Miller strapless satin gowns. Accordingly, it would have been wonderful to serve Barrack Vineyard's first-ever harvest to our wedding guests, but the grapes weren't ready. Instead, for our festivities, I arranged to have multiple cases of red and white wine bottled with custom-made labels reading *Marriage Merlot, Barrack Vineyards, Jodi and Sean Reserve.*

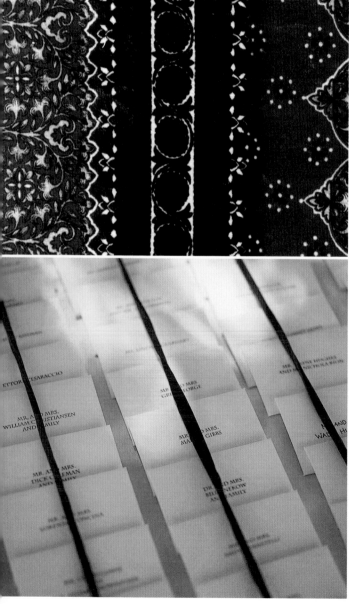

Dinner took us down another exotic back road. We decided to prepare an over-the-top extravagant Middle Eastern feast—a cornucopia of flavors, textures, spices, salads, and dips—and commissioned Wolfgang Puck from Spago to bring our fantasy to reality. As a tribute to Tom Barrack's love of all things Moroccan, Tom, Jodi, and I flew to Marrakech to gather inspiration and decoration for our party tent (not to mention our *after*-after-party tent). We had a fabulous time—and ended up shipping home crates filled with gorgeous-colored glass lanterns, comfy couches, seductive ottomans, lounge-ready pillows, shapely drinking glasses, authentic coffeepots, weirdly wonderful hookah pipes, and, best of all, an ornate Moroccan tent.

The night before the wedding, it was time to island-hop closer to home. Our destination was a local restaurant, where Sean's parents hosted an authentic Hawaiian luau, designed to help guests unwind and get to know one another before the next day's events. "Dress tropical," the invitations read, and in case any of our guests forgot, greeters were stationed by the doors to drape brightly colored, tropical floral leis around their shoulders. Inside, the restaurant had been transformed into a lush island extravaganza, with scented gardenias and a rainbow-colored mix of flower petals topping every table, while ukulele music serenaded guests in the background.

The next afternoon, we bid Hawaii farewell and strolled into the Middle East, by way of the Barrack family ranch. It was truly breathtaking!

At dusk, just as the mountains were beginning to darken, 350 guests motored down the Barracks' mile-long driveway, past wheat-colored pastures, sloping valleys, grazing horses, and the onset of a blearily golden late-afternoon light. As the guests reached the main residence, a team of valets in black tie intercepted them to relieve them of their cars and usher them along a tree-shaded path that led to the edge of the Barracks' beautiful polo fields. There, under umbrellas, and in between sips of fresh lemonade and bubbly sparkling water, family and friends took turns inscribing the guest book.

Next, accompanied by the soft strains of a flute quartet, Reverend Jeff Bridgeman, the wedding's officiant, escorted us to the center of the polo fields, where we took seats in comfortable wooden chairs. After the sizable wedding party—six bridesmaids, six groomsmen, the best man, the maid of honor, two adorable flower girls, and a ring bearer—made their way down the aisle, guests glanced at one another. Where was the bride? And her father? Nowhere to be seen. And then the crowd grew hushed.

We heard, echo-y and far away at first, then louder, the hollow, rhythmic *clip-clop* of horses' hooves, mixed with the faint jingling of a harness. Then we saw it: an old-fashioned wooden carriage in the distance, making a stately, drawn-out loop toward us. It was coming closer. Now we could make out the bride, seated beside her proudly smiling father, the carriage drawn by two handsome dark-brown, white-footed horses, each with a victory-garland of red roses around its neck.

This was a tender, lovely fairy-tale image, so simple and spellbinding that no one dared speak. The horse-drawn carriage creaked to a halt in front of the assembled guests. Tom Barrack descended, then held out his hand to Jodi, as she, too, carefully stepped down. The harness bells lightly jingled, but aside from a late-afternoon breeze, that was the only sound anyone could hear on a thousand acres. The bride's father bent down to straighten out his daughter's train, and then the two of them began slowly, gracefully making their way down the aisle.

It was all any of the guests could do to suppress their impulse to stand up and cheer. Jodi looked spectacular in an ivory silk-satin strapless Vera Wang wedding gown, her neck adorned with Martin Katz diamonds. Her hands enclosed a beautiful bouquet of red Black Magic roses. Now she took her place beside Sean underneath a beautiful arbor exquisitely festooned with willow branches, roses, and clusters of Concord grapes. It was time for the ceremony to begin.

This day, the Reverend Bridgeman reminded everyone, wasn't just for celebrating love between the bride and groom, but also the love among friends and family members.

Scripture readings. Prayers. The exchange of vows. The moment when Sean and Jodi placed rings around each other's fingers. The kiss. The moment the two turned to retrace their steps back up the aisle, this time as husband and wife. All those moments were locked in the minds and imaginations of all 350 guests. But if the buildup to the wedding had been both elemental and mythic, intimate and grand, now was the time for a seismic shift in mood, temperature, attitude—and pure momentum.

How else to explain the sudden streaming appearance of a red-robed gospel choir, feverishly lifting their voices to "Oh, Happy Day!"—a glorious, throw-your-head-back anthem that serenaded all the guests, by now helplessly clapping and singing along, from the arbor through a vast, stately pathway that led to the party tent. Admittedly, no one could take more than two steps before being met by one of the countless attentive waiters offering tall-stemmed glasses of Dom Pérignon, plus an exquisite array of appetizers straight from the Mediterranean: sumptuous black olives, crumbly feta, golden falafel, flaky *spanakopita*, delectable fried sheep's-milk cheese, and homemade stuffed grape leaves. The waiters' shadows streaked a pattern on the grass as they ushered guests toward the Bedouin-style tent now a thousand, now a hundred, now only ten yards away.

This ornate structure had heavy canvas sides with leather-trimmed edges that lifted to create a wraparound awning that evoked a Bedouin campground. Once inside, guests reveled in a richly exotic, sensuously aromatic wonderland. I'd dressed each of the eight exceptionally long tables with ecru linen, accented with crimson-and-grape-colored menus, beautiful red-and-gold-rimmed china perched on red-crystal chargers, exquisite arrays of ruby-toned flowers, moody amber candles, and beautiful silver bowls overflowing with fat ripe cherries, grapes, and kumquats.

If the forty-six-seat guest tables were a holiday-like celebration of red and gold, the bridal table was an all-white fairy-garden, with a spotless organza overlay, platinum-rimmed china and crystal, and gorgeous arrangements of huge white roses, punctuated overhead by votive chandeliers resembling angels' halos, multi-tiered in the middle, and single-tiered on either end.

Because of Jodi Barrack's love of family and heritage, we served our Middle Eastern feast family-style, starting off with bowls of richly grainy hummus, fresh calamari salad, *baba ghanoush,* marinated olives, *fattoush, tzatziki,* delicate carp roe, and *horiatiki*. Warm triangles of crispy pita bread accompanied all these dishes, as well as assorted flatbreads for dipping, tasting, sampling, and you-must-try-this sharing with neighbors. But this was merely the exotic warm-up for our main course: a succulent, cumin-infused roasted leg of lamb, accompanied by a Moroccan-style carrot compote, a colorful vegetable couscous, and zucchinis stuffed with rice. As a wonderful jazz trio played old-time supper music, two very important men made heartfelt toasts to the beautiful bride. After recalling his daughter as a little girl with a mass of unkempt brown curls, Tom Barrack added, movingly, "You're the most timeless tribute to beauty, grace, and elegance I have ever seen." There was not a dry eye in the house.

It was Sean's turn. It had been, he told the assembled guests, six years, eight months, thirty days, twelve hours, sixteen minutes, and eighteen seconds since the time Jodi first kissed him, adding, "I would not be anybody without you."

There was another gorgeous confection in store for the by-now-sated guests: a spectacular wedding cake concocted by Susan Halme of the Solvang Bakery, consisting of four tiers richly frosted with white buttercream, alternating with thick layers of locally grown red roses.

After the cake was cut and the guests served, it was time to . . . push things into the

"beyond" realm! The dinner canopy entrance was lifted, and a waitstaff now handsomely costumed in traditional Moroccan attire of black-and-gold-trimmed djellaba, fez, and pointed sandals ushered guests inside our second Bedouin-style tent, which Scheherazade herself could have imagined: a sexy oasis of dancing fountains, large lanterns, and canopied bars clad in gilded mirror, and topped off with overflowing bunches of yellow-green bananas. High-glam rouge-red seating areas shared room with ornate Moroccan sofas, rugs, coffee tables, and side chairs, additionally enhanced by hanging Moroccan lanterns, as well as palm trees. At every lounge table sat heaping bowls of nuts, dried fruits, and perfumed rose petals. Welcome to Marrakech, Casablanca, and all points in between!

To the melodies of the energetic band, the Sound Connection, Jodi and Sean hit the dance floor for a couple of numbers—then who should interrupt the festivities (and bring down the house) but a herd of colorfully costumed belly dancers, bursting across the stage and eventually convincing Jodi to join them in a shimmying belly-roll. Afterward, Jodi's bridesmaids joined her onstage to serenade the men in their lives with Shania Twain's "Man! I Feel Like a Woman!"

No one wanted to leave. Who in their right mind would? Yet we had one more bejeweled trick up our sleeves: the *after*-after-hours tent—small, black and white, also Moroccan-themed, its floors ankle-deep with dark-red and bright-pink rose petals. We had dedicated this tent to indulgence of the after-dinner variety: cigars, brandy, and exotic tobacco packed and smoked in snaky, traditional Moroccan hookahs. The tent could hold only fifteen people at a time, and by the time I reluctantly said my good-byes at two in the morning, the line to get in was virtually endless.

California. The Middle East. Wine, vineyards. An Old West horse-and-carriage. A bride's pride in her unusual heritage. All the elements came together to make what many guests later told Jodi wasn't just the best wedding they'd been to but a great, impossible-to-top party, and a gorgeous vintage celebration of family and love. Which is what weddings are, in the end, all about.

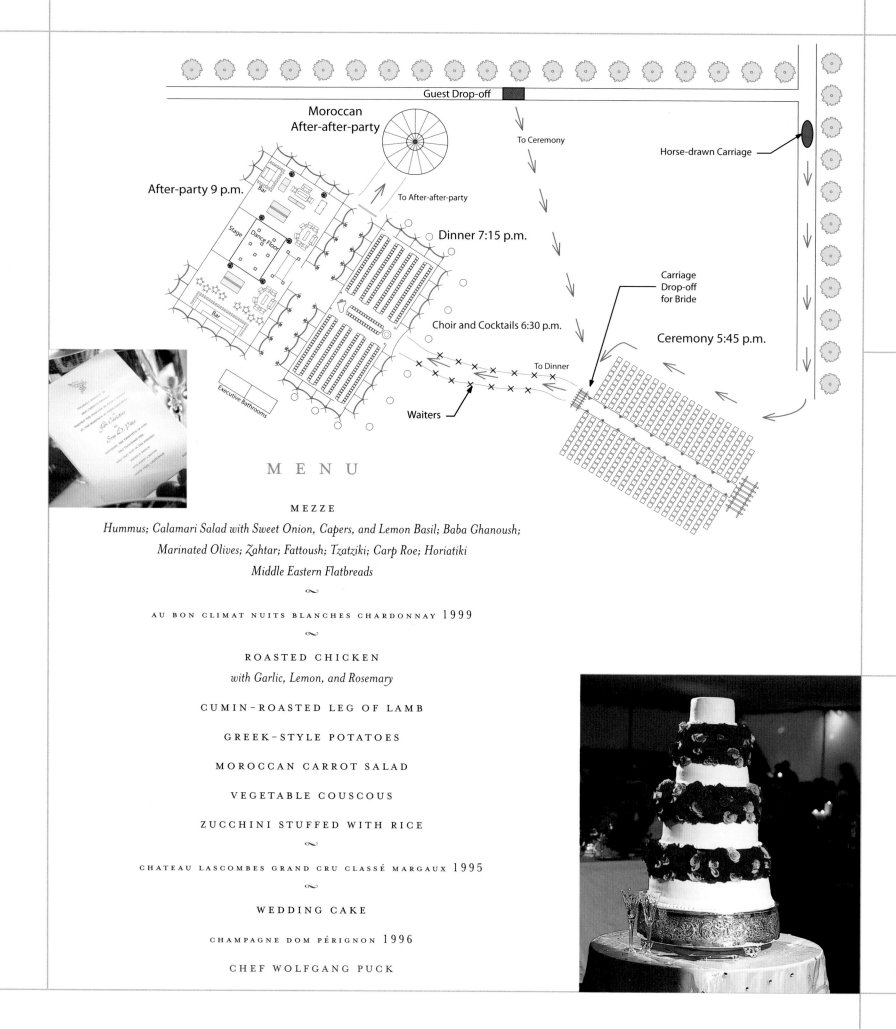

Guest Drop-off

Moroccan
After-after-party

To Ceremony

Horse-drawn Carriage

After-party 9 p.m.

Bar

To After-after-party

Stage | Dance Floor

Dinner 7:15 p.m.

Carriage
Drop-off
for Bride

Bar

Choir and Cocktails 6:30 p.m.

Ceremony 5:45 p.m.

Executive Bathrooms

To Dinner

Waiters

MENU

MEZZE

Hummus; Calamari Salad with Sweet Onion, Capers, and Lemon Basil; Baba Ghanoush;
Marinated Olives; Zahtar; Fattoush; Tzatziki; Carp Roe; Horiatiki
Middle Eastern Flatbreads

~

AU BON CLIMAT NUITS BLANCHES CHARDONNAY 1999

~

ROASTED CHICKEN

with Garlic, Lemon, and Rosemary

CUMIN-ROASTED LEG OF LAMB

GREEK-STYLE POTATOES

MOROCCAN CARROT SALAD

VEGETABLE COUSCOUS

ZUCCHINI STUFFED WITH RICE

~

CHATEAU LASCOMBES GRAND CRU CLASSÉ MARGAUX 1995

~

WEDDING CAKE

CHAMPAGNE DOM PÉRIGNON 1996

CHEF WOLFGANG PUCK

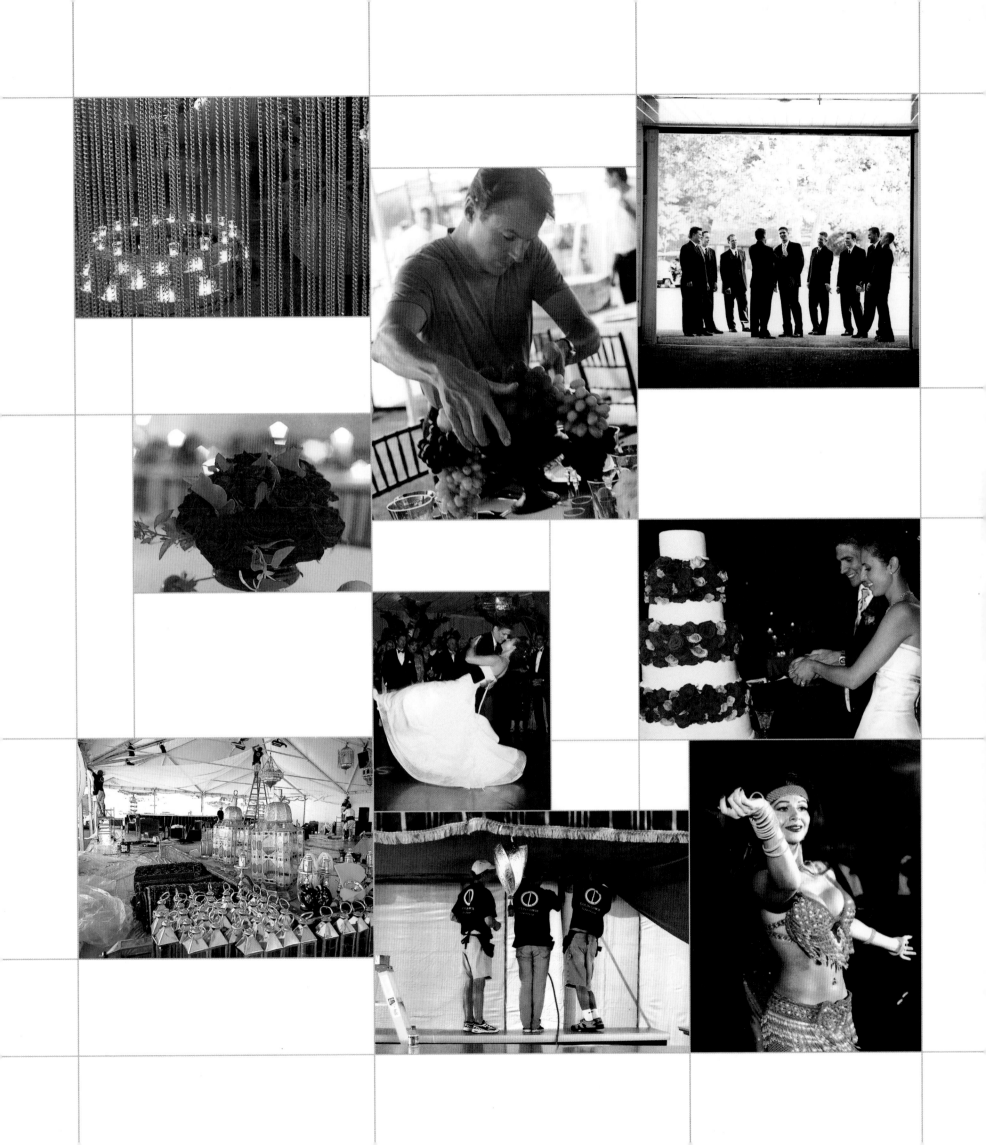

THE ROOTS OF A GREAT AFFAIR

Many people spend a lot of time escaping from who they are. But there's a lot to be said for proudly embracing your identity, and incorporating family traditions into your festivities. Not only does this communicate to your guests where you come from, it also grounds you in the best of the past. And it makes for a wedding that's festive, one of a kind, and truly memorable.

I'm not suggesting you go overboard. Instead, hand-pick a few traditional family elements that strike you as distinctive, special, and emblematic, and weave them into the food, the decor, the music, the invitations, or the wedding ceremony itself. If you're in doubt, ask your parents or grandparents. They might be able to regale you with tales about a few forgotten customs, come up with some fabulous family dishes—or even tell you what your ancestors did during *their* weddings.

Since the landscape of weddings has changed so much today—there are more interracial and intercultural weddings than ever before—it's important to extract the best rituals of both backgrounds to share with your guests. That way, these customs become a common denominator for all.

HERE ARE A FEW IDEAS

Incorporate a family motif—a coat of arms, an Irish or Scottish plaid, or some other distinctive family totem—into the wedding invitations.

Treat your guests to a traditional song before, during, or after the ceremony.

Serve a spectacular family recipe during cocktail hour, dinner, or dessert.

Accentuate a family ritual during the reception— maybe a folk dance or a familiar toast.

Let your party favor reflect your roots. Send guests home with a gift or a token, large or small, that has family associations, or that can only be found where your family hails from.

TO ITALY, WITH LOVE

Erica Holton and Antonio Reid

CAPRI, ITALY

JUNE 10, 2000

The island of Capri, on the Amalfi Coast of Italy, is one of the sexiest, most romantic destinations in the world. It came as no surprise that music-industry executive Antonio "L.A." Reid, and his beautiful bride, Erica Holton, had both left their hearts there several months earlier. On that visit, Antonio and Erica were at a seaside restaurant in Anacapri, when Antonio gently removed a stunning emerald-cut engagement ring from his pocket and, leaning across the table, requested Erica's hand in marriage.

Where do you find a perfect location *within* a perfect location? During a preliminary scouting trip, Erica and I decided upon the beautiful Capri Palace Hotel, in Anacapri (the most unspoiled part of the island), approximately a thousand feet above the open Mediterranean Sea and the Gulf of Naples. From my first glimpse of the white hotel lobby, which exuded an airy, modern elegance, I knew it would 100 percent complement the cool and dash of the newlyweds' sensibilities. The recently renovated hotel was a gorgeous mix-and-match of the cutting edge and the classical, a mélange of Mediterranean architecture, Louis XVI–style furniture, majolica and stone tile, and miles of luxurious white draperies drifting and billowing in the wind. With the Capri Palace as our backdrop, I had no doubt the results would be breathtaking—and we hadn't even begun planning the wedding itself yet.

My palette for the wedding would be coral—and fittingly, I created two separate coral shades, one darker (a terra-cotta tone) and one lighter (a salmon tone), set against white. Stationery designers Margot Madison and Cindy Loon came up with a fabulous save-the-date card and invitation that evoked to a T the rocky, exotic, sunlit essence of Capri: three die-cut paper sculptures, one for each day of our upcoming weekend, each a different shade of our coral palette, all three mirroring the jaggedly cut turrets of the Caprian coastline, and with a response card stylishly tucked into a background slot. The ink ranged from cream on our darker paper to a rich burgundy adorning our lighter stock, and the typestyle had a playfully Gothic feel. The envelopes were finished off in coral, with ecru calligraphy and a jagged-edged flap inspired by the silhouette of the island.

While guests were at home dealing with RSVPs, Erica, my production crew, and I

returned to Capri, where we met with my friend Tonino Cacace, the owner and host of the Capri Palace, who took us on an extravagant tour of the ancient, sensuously sunlit isle. Along the way, he showed off the essence of off-the-beaten-track Capri: little churches like crumbling jewels; tiny snaky streets; fabulous shops; restaurants at the bottom of a thousand old stairs; and a local florist whose spectacular blooms we would later use in our ceremony.

As always, a well-informed guest is a happy guest. The confirmation packages we sent outlined all the details of our upcoming Capri weekend, including the three-day itinerary, travel arrangements, and the dress code, all neatly arranged inside a handsomely engraved folder, with an old world–style map of Capri as the cover illustration, and tied with a dark coral grosgrain ribbon. When the weekend arrived, staff members attired in ANTONIO & ERICA shirts and caps were waiting at the docks to greet the new arrivals. No worries! That same well-cared-for feeling continued when guests entered their hotel suites to find "R"-embroidered welcome bags, each containing a bottle of locally made Limoncello liqueur, suntan lotion, a few fabulous CDs, a scented candle, a beach sarong, and a welcome note and itinerary of the weekend's events.

If life gives you lemons, why not create a lemon-themed rehearsal dinner? One of my favorite restaurants in Capri, the utterly charming Da Paolina, happens to be located inside and under a giant fragrant lemon grove. I dressed Da Paolina's tables to the floor in beautiful sage-green linen, with sage-green napkins tied with lengths of twine. Everywhere was simple white china, with hand-painted lemon accents, bowls spilling over with ripe lemons, and in each table's center a tall lemon topiary, surrounded by emerald-green votive candles. Our chairs were custom-cushioned in a lemon-patterned fabric, and even our waiters were clad in bright yellow shirts and lemon-patterned vests. What a shock I got when I realized that the shirt I was wearing matched the waiters' vests!

I am not typically a big buffet fan, but the incredible, colorful, famously fresh buffet that Da Paolina lays out is one of my favorite spreads in the world. Where to start? Antipasto; succulent tomatoes; marinated vegetables; crumbly local cheeses; soft white mozzarellas; just-caught calamari, squid, and prawns; as well as all varieties of braised, grilled, and steamed local fish. Musicians in striped shirts strolled languorously from table to table, cheerfully crooning Italian folk songs, and making it feel almost illegal not to join in for a chorus. Da Paolino's intimacy, its musicians, and its whimsical, lemony decor made it the ideal icebreaker for Antonio's and Erica's families.

After dinner, guests headed to the La Taverna nightclub to dance the night away—and then it was on to the local VIP nightclub, Taverna Anema e Core, world-famous for enticing the most straitlaced guests to let their guard (and hair) down as they sing along to the club's legendary guitar-strumming emcee, Guido.

The next day was devoted to rest, recovery, lounging, shopping, and pampering. Many guests made a beeline for the incredible Capri Beauty Farm, adjacent to the hotel, for facials, wraps, and luxurious massages. We'd also arranged for guided tours of Villa San Michele, the Blue Grotto, Pompeii, Sorrento, and the Amalfi Coast—as well as to Capri's countless fabulous shops and restaurants (including La Capannina, home to the world's best stuffed zucchini blossoms). By the late afternoon, everybody was rested, and ready for the romance of a beautiful wedding.

At sunset, our guests—by now elegantly attired in white linen—took their seats in the upper rooftop garden of the Capri Palace, overlooking the ocean. I'd hand-painted a canvas runner in a terra-cotta ivy pattern (to complement the tile floor), which I further adorned with scads of white rose petals. Two enormous and elaborate arbors, draped with coral and blush roses, stood at the top and bottom of the aisle. Beyond these two arbors floated the to-die-for vista of the Mediterranean, the sky a swirling cluster of pink, orange, and purple, the water a deepening blue-black. Scoring this heavenly scene was a six-member classical orchestra from Naples, who gently serenaded our guests with Bach and Handel adagios and orchestral suites. You have no idea what an ordeal it was to get them—and their instruments—from Naples to Capri by boat . . . and then up the mountain to the Capri Palace. But it was worth it.

To the melody of Beethoven's "Romance," Erica made her way down the runner in a simple, beautiful Vera Wang wedding gown, its bodice and hemline trimmed in lace. I'd designed her veil myself, using a large oval piece of silk tulle, heavily embroidered on both ends to match and accentuate the beading of her gown. Diamanté and pearl pins from Alexandre de Paris secured the veil to Erica's hair. After the ceremony, she removed the veil from her hair, and later looped it delicately around her shoulders as a wrap when the temperatures fell during dinner.

As she proceeded through the second arbor to the first and was greeted by the reverend

and by her groom, Paola Tedesco of the Naples Opera House sang a hauntingly beautiful version of "Avé Maria." Next, the newlyweds' two mothers came forward, and as one, lit a unity candle, whose light they then passed along to Erica and Antonio. The gorgeous bride passed her light along to Antonio's young children from his first marriage. Now Erica and Antonio made their way down opposite sides of the aisles, leaning over to illuminate their guests' candles as well. So as the sun was going down, all our guests were holding slender white candles that were alight. It was a magical moment when Erica and Antonio returned to the arbor to take their vows under the spiritual illumination of their families and friends. We were united by wind, water, and fire, by the sunset, by friendship, by family and ritual, and mostly, by the love we were witnessing between the bride and groom.

Following the vows, the band played Mendelssohn's "Wedding March" as guests filtered over to the cocktail area, where they were met by waiters serving mother-of-pearl teaspoons of Beluga caviar, fried and stuffed zucchini blossoms (we'd re-created La Capannina's amazing signature dish), and wonderful *suppli* (fried rice balls), washed down with magnums of Rosé Taittinger Champagne—while the San Carlo Orchestra played jazzy, upbeat swing and standards. After cocktails, it was time to retire downstairs for dinner.

The band, Soulville, was already swinging and jiving on the edge of our huge round white dance floor but paused to introduce "The new Mr. and Mrs. Antonio Reid," before inviting all married couples present to join the newlyweds for the first dance, the Louis Armstrong classic "What a Wonderful World." Afterward, guests (married, single, whatever!) took their seats at tables swathed in beautiful, lavishly bordered white embroidery woven with a dark coral sea-vine pattern and trimmed in dark coral silk ribbon. Adjacent tables were done identically, in a lighter salmon color. Our head table was dressed in white-on-white, of the same vine-patterned cloth, so it would stand distinct from the others. The chairs themselves were white, slipcovered and cushy, with dark coral piping, and a regal "R" on each seat-back. Each one of our white overscaled napkins was also embroidered with a stylish "R." On every tip dangled a piece of good-luck coral nestled in eighteen-carat gold. (When guests lifted their napkins, the menu peeked out from underneath.) For our centerpieces, thick doughnuts of Madeline, Sonia, and Silva roses, in shades of cream, coral, and terra-cotta, surrounded three-wicked candles in glimmering glass hurricanes.

The room was a flickering sea of gold votive candles. It was time to dine. Gnocchi in fresh San Marzano tomato sauce. Creamy risotto with porcini mushrooms. Penne with shrimp. The best Tuscan filets of beef you've ever tasted. Crunchy roasted potatoes. Rosemary-infused chicken. An unforgettable local eggplant, tomato, and mozzarella dish, followed by a palate-cleansing arugula-and-radicchio salad dusted with freshly shaved Parmesan. As Erica and Antonio were cutting the cake—a masterpiece of elaborate (and edible) coral roses—guests quietly sipped Sgroppinos, a famous cocktail from the Cipriani in Venice, made from vodka, Prosecco, and lemon sorbet, served in beautiful champagne flutes, and finished with a sprig of mint.

After dinner and dancing, a huge set of draperies opened, inviting guests into the hotel lounge, which I had lit with hundreds of sunset-orange votive candles. There we served an extravagant array of chocolates, biscotti, bowls of cherries, mini-pastries, coffee, grappa, and cigars. Our guests, clad in white linen, sipping cognac and savoring cigars, looked as though they could have stepped out of a fifties movie—sophisticated, sexy, and cool.

Guests could have danced all night—and did—pausing only near midnight to commemorate Erica's grandmother's seventy-eighth birthday with a small, candlelit cake. At some point, Erica and Antonio slipped back to their hotel room, which was now ankle-deep in rose petals and lushly lit with 150 votives, one for every guest at the wedding.

MENU

TRIO OF PASTA
Gnocchi with Tomato Sauce, Risotto with Porcini Mushrooms,
Penne with Prawns

JERMANN PINOT BIANCO 1998

∾

TUSCAN BEEF IN MADEIRA WINE SAUCE

ROASTED POTATOES

EGGPLANT WITH TOMATO AND MOZZARELLA

∾

ANTINORI TIGNANELLO 1997

SGROPPINOS

∾

ARUGULA AND RADICCHIO SALAD
with Parmesan Cheese

∾

WEDDING CAKE

Ceremony on Roof Deck
Overlooking Mediterranean
6 p.m.

Ocean

Guest
Entry

Bar

White
Dance
Floor

Band

Main Table

Guest Entry

Dinner and After-party
7 p.m.

ZEN AND THE ART OF THE PRE-REHEARSAL

Imagine. You're a bride. You've just gotten married, and now it's time for dinner. At the bridal table, the handsome waiter brings over an entrée and sets it before you. "But that's not how I thought it would be!" you hear yourself exclaim.

No one can deny that there are countless ways to assemble a Caesar salad or arrange a platter of sashimi. Some people are hooked on nouveau cuisine; others want to serve their guests something heartier. How can you ensure that you and the catering staff are on the same page—or in this case, plate?

There's only one fail-safe way I know of: Stage a complete "dress rehearsal" of your meal, so there are no mishaps, miscommunications, or surprises. If everything's in sync, you can feel free to sit back, relax, let go, and enjoy the evening. If not, you can fix it then and there.

TABLE

Set the table with the printed menu, the linens, the silver, and the crystal. How does it look, not just singly, but all together? Is this the impression you're aiming for? How do these objects feel in your hands?

Have your florist create the precise floral centerpiece with candles that you'll be using on your wedding day. Does it overpower the table? Is it too skimpy? Can your guests see one another across the table? Are you happy with the flower choices and quantities?

Sample every course, from the salad to the entrée to the dessert, and if something isn't to your liking, say so. Most chefs appreciate a little constructive criticism, and they are there to make you happy. By all means, ask for a re-tasting to ensure that each course is exactly as you want it.

Taste all the wines along with the courses they'll be accompanying. Do they complement the food? If not, replace them.

Sit on the exact chair on which your guests will be seated. Is it comfortable? Too big, too small, too hard, too low to the ground? Are the seats too close together at the table to allow for adequate elbow room?

Take notes (and even photographs) of the sample table during the run-through so you can revisit them later on, then communicate your wishes to the banquet planner.

SUGAR AND SPICE AND EVERYTHING FABULOUS

Marja Allen and Jean-Georges Vongerichten

NEW YORK CITY

SEPTEMBER 22, 2004

He came, he cooked, he conquered. Jean-Georges Vongerichten hit New York in the 1980s, reinventing the notion of haute cuisine by substituting vegetable juices and infused oils for butter and cream sauces, and introducing Asian ingredients such as ginger and lemongrass into the culinary patois. Along the way, he opened a series of red-hot restaurants, authored best-selling cookbooks, and used his classical training to come up with America's answer to nouvelle cuisine. Even better for me, he and I became good friends.

The only thing more exhilarating, more magical, more fantastic than planning a wedding is . . . planning a wedding for two people you adore. So, when Jean-Georges announced that he and his girlfriend of six years, actress Marja Allen, were finally going to tie the knot, and then asked me to help with the celebration, I couldn't have been happier. I defy anyone to spend thirty seconds with this couple and not fall madly in love. The only thing more beautiful than Marja's face is her heart, which is roughly the size of Central Park.

Not only was I thrilled to be involved in the union of such a well-suited pair, but I also looked forward to the endlessly interesting possibilities their heritages—his French, hers a mix of African-American, Korean, and Native American—would offer us for inspiration. Both are spiritual people, and they knew that they wanted an intimate marriage ceremony for just immediate family and close friends (about sixty people in all). But Marja and Jean-Georges also love a good party, so we needed to figure out a way to expand the celebration to include 180 more people after the "I dos" were said and done.

We didn't have to go very far to discover the right venue—we were sitting in it! Jean-Georges's Asian restaurant, Spice Market, located in Manhattan's fashionable Meatpacking District, would prove to be the ideal spot for the reception. We could hold an intimate private ceremony on the roof of the ultrachic six-floor boutique hotel Soho House, located right next door, and then host a blessing, reception dinner, and after-party for another 180 guests downstairs in the exotic, opulent atmosphere of Spice Market. The rooftop terrace would be a gorgeous spot for the type of ceremony Marja and Jean-Georges wanted, enveloping their cherished families, blending their beloved cultures, and placing them smack in the heart of where they lived, worked, and fell in love.

The ceremony was set for early evening, overlooking the Manhattan skyline. On one side of the roof, we constructed an intimate canopied tent, draping the ceiling and walls in shades of cream and camel. We covered the floors with an understated sisal carpet. The flowers were done in deep, rich shades of cinnamon and wine—an elegant reflection of autumn. Rustic stands topped with hurricane candles and wreaths of sable-brown Leonidas roses, Vendela roses, Lemone roses, berries, magnolia leaves, hanging amaranthus, red tea leaves, and green hydrangeas lined the aisles, and an elaborate arch made from the same array of flowers marked the entranceway. I left open the side of the tent facing the Hudson River, because very little in life rivals the shadows of the September sun setting behind the Manhattan skyline. Add to that the soft, subtle shades of the canopy and the warm butterscotch and deep-apricot blush of the setting sun, and you have the stuff that dreams are made of—ethereal, sensuous, and romantic as a first kiss.

The guests' chairs were arranged in a semicircular formation around an S-shaped aisle. I chose a serpentine pathway to maximize Marja's walk toward her groom and to create the feeling that she was strolling among her family and friends, rather than past them. It not only added that extra degree of intimacy we had all been striving for but it also gave Jean-Georges an extra moment to take in the ravishing woman he was about to join in holy matrimony. Marja looked luminous in a Carolina Herrera ivory satin top and sleek beaded skirt as her father escorted her down the aisle and proceeded to give his adored little girl away.

In the end, it's not the grandeur of the setting but the content of the ceremony that elevates a wedding from lovely to mythical. During the planning stages, I had arranged for Marja and Jean-Georges to meet with an extraordinary woman whom I consider a colleague, a friend, and a spiritual guide—Dr. Linda Garbett. She's performed many weddings for clients of mine all over the world, and I knew she would be a great match for this couple. Linda specializes in creating exceptionally personal ceremonies that rely heavily on symbolism and cultural references. Not everyone is open to this type of wedding; some prefer a more traditional approach. But I knew that Linda would be able to capture exactly the feeling Marja and Jean-Georges wanted to convey.

Linda has a fascinating way of putting everyone in the room on exactly the same spiritual plane. She strikes a chord between the personal and the universal, so while her words are directed toward the bride and groom, it seems as if they're meant for each and every soul in attendance. She is also a great believer in using ritual to pay homage to heritage: Before the guests had even arrived, Linda burned sage to cleanse the area of any unfriendly spirits (a Native American custom). After Marja's father had escorted his daughter down the aisle, Linda had both sets of parents come forward to ceremonially wash their children's hands as a last act of parental duties (an African tradition). And as an ode to the long line of French bakers in Jean-Georges's family, she had the groom bake a loaf of bread and present it as an offering to Marja's parents, who shared it with everyone in attendance. All of these gestures brought the ceremony to life, but it was the story Linda told of how Marja and Jean-Georges met, how their relationship slowly evolved, and how their dear friends supported and nurtured their union, that left guests holding hands and reaching for their tissues.

As soon as Linda pronounced the bride and groom husband and wife, it was time for champagne—a chilled jeroboam of Veuve Clicquot La Grande Dame Rosé, to be specific. I cut off the top of the bottle with a saber, a dramatic gesture few guests were expecting! It took a little extra time, but it made for over-the-top theater, *plus* we needed those extra minutes for Marja, Jean-Georges, and Linda to go downstairs and change for the next phase of the wedding celebration.

But before I begin to describe the next phase of our celebration, let me back up and explain a little more about why I knew Spice Market was the very best venue for my friends. Of course, the restaurant has tremendous meaning for Jean-Georges, as it is part of his life's work, and for Marja, who spends a lot of time there entertaining VIP guests. But it's the dazzling look of the place that so utterly captured the style of both the bride and groom. The interior is stunning—it's a street scene from Southeast Asia. Just about every inch is adorned in artifacts shipped from there. Yet the exclusive use of wood for the decor, the burnished peach lighting, and the vertical architecture each visually scale down the size of the restaurant to cozier proportions, providing a marvelous sense of privacy.

For our next set of events, I went in armed with a single color that would build upon what was already a sumptuous backdrop. The color orange never fails to create a fiery, fairy-tale setting. In this case, it was just the right color to pull together the look we were going for. First, we cleared out all the furniture from the main level and set up long tables to accommodate our 240 dinner guests. Next, I went to town decorating: We embellished the existing

curtains with sheer layers of mango organza and bordered them with garlands of saffron marigolds. The tables were covered with tangerine silk and Indian embroidered and beaded overlays. The napkins and chair slipcovers—all hand-embroidered—were also done in mango, saffron, and orange. Amber glassware, bronze chargers, and centerpieces filled with yellow roses, orange dahlias, and small orange berries complemented the tabletop fabrics. The six-tiered cake, created by New York City–based "sugar artist extraordinaire" Margaret Braun, followed suit, adorned with hand-painted flowers in shades of persimmon, pink, coppery pink, and fuchsia with gold piping. One final special touch: I arranged to have male ushers dressed in saffron-colored saris greet guests at the door. Think Bombay Bride meets 2004.

The glory of our setting demanded that we come up with a bit of theater for the blessing itself. Taking advantage of the bi-level design of the restaurant, we created a path for the procession that was ankle-deep in rose petals through the main floor and down the open central staircase that led to the restaurant's lower level, with a cupola halfway down that we draped with garlands of white orchids, tuberose blossoms, and faceted crystals. We set up this beautiful cupola in between the two landings, so guests could watch both from downstairs and from above overlooking the railings. The sari-clad men who had greeted guests led off the procession ringing a Burmese gong that Linda had had shipped to New York. Along the way, they lit the tall Florentine candelabras that lined the aisle—each with about twenty candles. When the candelabras flamed an exultant topaz, Jean-Georges came down the aisle, followed by Marja—the groom in a contemporary taupe suit, and the bride in a Reem Acra peach-beige silk off-the-shoulder gown embroidered in antique gold. The scene reached its peak when Marja arrived under the cupola. There she stood, like an angel bathed in white light and surrounded by those curtains of white orchids and crystals. To say she looked gorgeous would definitely be an understatement—neither does *breathtaking* begin to describe it.

The blessing itself was as moving and meaningful as the rooftop ceremony. Drawing heavily on Marja's Korean roots, Linda orchestrated a series of different traditional Korean wedding blessings. At one point, Jean-Georges presented a carved wooden goose, called a *kirogi,* to Marja's mother, a symbol of his faithfulness to Marja (geese famously mate for life).

At another point, the couple signified the permanence of their vows by circling each other linked by a long strand of infinity beads looped in a figure eight around their shoulders. But the highlight of the ceremony was the sharing of a special white wine with a special wedding vow known in Korea as *kubere*. The wine was poured into cups made from two halves of a gourd and presented to Jean-Georges and Marja by Marja's mother. The bride and groom sipped from their separate cups, and then the wine was mixed together, poured once more into the gourd cups, and sipped again. Guests who hadn't been at the actual wedding still had the honor of watching this couple blend their lives together . . . and needless to say, it was once again time to take out the handkerchiefs.

With emotions still running high from the two ceremonies we'd just witnessed, we brought everyone upstairs to the restaurant for a family-style wedding feast. The menu—featuring all the Spice Market delicacies—was beyond the beyond. For the first course, we served small beggar's purses stuffed with caviar. The second-course menu alone was to die for. It included (but believe me when I say, was not limited to) shaved tuna with chili tapioca, chicken and coconut milk soup, Vietnamese spring rolls, pork satay, and spiced chicken samosas. For their main course, guests gorged on succulent steamed lobster with a butter,

fried garlic, and ginger chili sauce, red curried duck, and grilled Niman Ranch strip steak with garlic, coriander, and sesame. Dessert, of course, was a scrumptious slice of Margaret's confectionary masterpiece, dense chocolate with a mocha-praline filling, served with a choice of sorbets and ice creams in cardboard take-out containers.

It wasn't until almost midnight that guests finished dining and drinking and Marja and Jean-Georges invited everyone back downstairs for the after-party. During dinner, my team had transformed the blessing site into a fabulous nightclub, adding copious candles, a tufted gold leather bar with a starburst mirror attached to the front, and white leather sofas and seating pods. At the center of the room we'd constructed an elevated dance floor, and the nooks around the perimeter of the room were perfect for people to mellow out with drinks and talk. The effect was both groovy and sophisticated—a club anyone would love to be a VIP member of. The guests were thrilled as renowned deejay Stephane Pompougnac, of the Hotel Costes in Paris, spun tunes for what became an all-night bash. At three A.M. we passed trays of miniature hamburgers for anyone with a case of predawn munchies (they also counterbalanced some of the alcohol!) as Stephane spun on, guests laughed and partied, and Jean-Georges held Marja tightly and danced the hours away.

MENU

VEUVE CLICQUOT LA GRANDE DAME ROSÉ

COCKTAILS AND GINGER MARGARITAS

LOUIS ROEDERER CRISTAL 1997 OR GINGER MARGARITA

OSETRA CAVIAR BEGGAR'S PURSES

SHAVED TUNA
with Chili Tapioca, Asian Pear, and Lime

CHICKEN AND COCONUT MILK SOUP

VIETNAMESE SPRING ROLLS

PORK SATAY
with Pickled Vegetables

BLACK PEPPER SHRIMP
with Sun-Dried Pineapple

CHARRED CHILI-RUBBED BEEF SKEWER

SPICED CHICKEN SAMOSAS
with Cilantro Yogurt

GREEN PAPAYA SALAD, CHARRED LONG BEANS,
Crystallized Ginger, and Tamarind

CRUNCHY SQUID SALAD
with Ginger, Papaya, and Cashews

STEAMED LOBSTER
with Butter, Fried Garlic, Ginger, and Dried Chili

HALIBUT CHA CA LA VONG
with Herb Salad

BABY CORN AND BROCCOLI
with Lemongrass and Chili

GRILLED NIMAN RANCH STRIP STEAK
with Garlic, Coriander, and Sesame

CHAR-GRILLED CHICKEN
with Kumquats in a Lemongrass Dressing

RED CURRIED DUCK

VEGETABLES IN GREEN CURRY

GINGER FRIED RICE

∞

PAUL ET FILS BLANCK PATERGARTEN PINOT GRIS 2003

∞

KISTLER CHARDONNAY 2002

∞

ROBERT SINSKEY VINEYARDS FOUR VINEYARDS PINOT NOIR 2000

∞

WEDDING CAKE
Assorted Sorbets and Ice Creams

BILLECART-SALMON PREMIER CRU ROSÉ

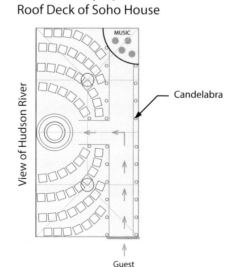

Ceremony 6 p.m.
Roof Deck of Soho House

View of Hudson River

Candelabra

Guest
Entry

MUSIC

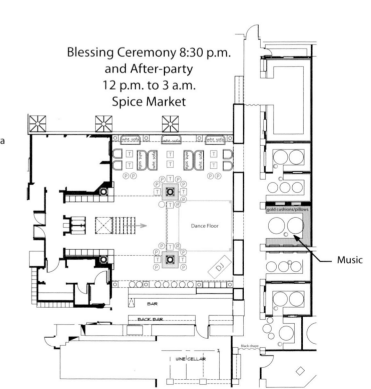

Blessing Ceremony 8:30 p.m.
and After-party
12 p.m. to 3 a.m.
Spice Market

Dance Floor

Music

Dinner 9:30 p.m.
Upstairs at Spice Market

Main Table

Groom

Downstairs to
Blessing Ceremony

OPEN TO BELOW

Bride

BAR

WINE ROOM

COATS

UP

Guest
Entry

9TH AVE.

13TH STREET

CREATING YOUR OWN CEREMONY

More and more, I run into couples who want to opt out of the traditional wedding ceremony. Instead, they're choosing unique settings, a more personal format, and multicultural flourishes. I'm all for it. It's an absolute pleasure for me to create a fabulous reception filled with personal touches, but the ceremony itself is what the wedding is really about. Why not get married the way you want to? It's your day.

Dr. Linda Garbett has officiated at many of my clients' weddings over the years. She loves to work with couples to incorporate the spiritual and the personal into a ceremony that's completely one of a kind. If you're thinking of creating your very own "I dos," keep some of her tips in mind:

Choose vows that work for you. People think that they need to write and say their own vows to make a wedding personal. Not necessarily so. Linda finds that many of the couples she works with prefer that she take the reigns and write the vows for them. They even prefer that she *say* them. It frees the couple up to listen, and it takes away the pressure of having to "perform" in front of a crowd at one of the most important moments of their lives. If you do decide to write and recite your own vows, be sure to practice in advance.

If you're working with an officiant, set up a meeting beforehand to find out if he or she is willing to think outside the box. Some officiants are, others aren't. Another option: Ask a close personal friend to officiate (it's a breeze to become licensed for the day). "This is becoming an increasingly popular way to go," says Linda. "Couples want someone to officiate who really knows them."

Draw on your ethnicity. As Linda did for Marja and Jean-Georges's big day, include rituals that incorporate one or both of your backgrounds. You can research just about any type of wedding ritual on the Internet, as well as order any props you might need (such as the wooden goose used in Marja and Jean-Georges's blessing). Not only will these rituals add meaning to your ceremony, they also add beautiful visual flourishes.

Involve your guests. There are many ways to do this. You can have the officiant incorporate people by name into the speech. Or you can try what one couple did at their wedding: The bride and groom included a ribbon with the invitation and asked that everyone write a message on it and return it with the response card. The ribbons were then displayed at the wedding ceremony for all to read. (Having each guest come up to light a candle gets tedious fast. The trick to involving guests is to choose a gesture that doesn't logistically bog down your ceremony.)

BAREFOOT ON THE BEACH

Sandra Goff and Andrew Farkas

PARADISE ISLAND, THE BAHAMAS

January 14, 2001

What do you give to a wedding guest who has everything? In the case of Andrew Farkas and his bride, Sandra Goff, the answer was easy: simplicity. A beautiful Bahamian beach. White sand under bare feet. The heavenly sounds of a fifty-member gospel choir. A to-die-for wedding feast, followed by a red-hot dance party. Together, it all added up to a wedding weekend that was casually chic, elegant in the old Caribbean style, and totally unforgettable.

In civilian life, Andrew is a hardworking businessman, the CEO of one of the largest commercial and residential real-estate companies in the world. Off duty, he's a passionate man who's most at home among the elements: sky, sand, water, sunlight, his boat, and the gleam of Paradise Island in the Bahamas. He shares his love of the outdoors with Sandi, a screenwriter whom he met on a blind date through their fitness trainer. Neither of them expected anything more than friendship to come out of that first meeting, much less romance and enduring love.

Andrew and Sandi had a single vision for their wedding. It should be fun, casual, utterly non-nerve-racking—but also elegant and traditional, a nod to the glorious Colonial heritage of the Bahamas. For their guests, Andrew and Sandi wanted the three-day wedding weekend getaway to feel like an uninterrupted dream, a fantasy-respite from life. Paradise Island is all about sunlight, heat, water, and miles of pristine white sand. Little wonder that Andrew and Sandi wanted to take their wedding vows on the beach, barefoot, with family members and close friends as witnesses.

When it came time to pick out the perfect wedding site, there was no doubt in their minds. Two years earlier, on Valentine's Day, Andrew and Sandi had fallen in love with Paradise Island's sumptuous Ocean Club. Together, the three of us flew down to the Bahamas on a preliminary scouting trip. Having once planned the opening party for the nearby Atlantis Resort, I was well-versed with the Ocean Club and its surrounding properties. I wanted to create a fantastic, over-the-top wedding that satisfied Andrew and Sandi's desire to mix and match the classic formality of the old with the outdoorsy informality of the new.

My inspiration—"Colonial Beach"—fit the Ocean Club perfectly. Though sporty and contemporary, it also recalls a Bahamas from long ago. Breezy verandas and airy terraces adorn each of the club's buildings. The manicured lawns are dotted with fountain courtyards, marble sculptures, and even a resplendent twelfth-century Augustinian cloister. The Ocean Club's intricate thirty-five-acre garden, modeled after the grounds of Versailles, peers up and over the breathtaking blue-green of the Caribbean.

Since Andrew and Sandi are devoted sailors and unapologetic fun-seekers—their boat, the *Kaori*, owes its name to the couple's favorite brand of sake—I came up with another idea. We would sail the *Kaori* and its crew to the nearby marina and ask the captain to officiate the wedding there. The captain, who's known the groom for nine years, leapt at the chance.

Every great party starts off with a great invitation, and New York stationer Ellen Weldon came up with a divinely inspiring choice. Framing hardy ecru stock and sepia brown ink within fine, delicate Japanese caning paper (it resembles rattan), she created a tri-fold, which she then bound with a sumptuous hand-dyed ribbon. Every single piece of paper from Andrew and Sandi's wedding weekend, from the welcome-notes in guests' hotel rooms, to the menus, to the seating cards, was embossed with a simple scallop shell.

In mid-January, as wintry weather blasted most of the United States, 150 wedding guests descended on beautiful, blue-skied Paradise Island. That first night, William and Karen Lauder, two of Andrew and Sandi's closest friends, hosted a jubilant Caribbean welcome feast. Originally slated to be held on Atlantis's Cove beach, the festivities were shifted poolside when the weather turned overcast. The change of venue hardly mattered. I'd decorated the tables with cream-and-white sarongs, each one bearing a simple shell motif. Atop every table were clusters of white tropical orchids and old-fashioned hurricane lamps. The dress code? "Fun and Festive." Guests mingled, serving themselves from a scattering of buffet stations, including an icily sumptuous raw bar laid out in the hold of an antique rowboat; in addition there was barbecued chicken, local seafood, native lobster, and even a thirty-pound grouper, custom-carved by an island chef. Local islanders adorned in Bahamian dress welcomed the guests with trays of tropical cocktails.

After a refreshing night's sleep, it was time for the wedding day.

We awoke the next morning to an agitated sky and gusty winds. But as the time for the ceremony drew closer, the clouds brightened and lifted, the gale force calmed down, and the Bahamian sun emerged from hiding. By late in the afternoon, the sky was gently lit in sorbetlike streaks of light pink, mellow orange, and yellowy gilt, all mirrored off the darkening tides. Rabbi Judy Lewis, who would be officiating at the ceremony, gave voice to what everybody was thinking: that God had fashioned a picture-perfect backdrop for the soon-to-be newlyweds.

We'd asked that all the guests dress in white. This may seem restrictive (and even a little pushy), but consider what a pleasure it is to put together an elegant outfit, especially for a friend's wedding. The dress code unites perfect strangers. It creates a feeling of solidarity. It sets everyone on a collective mission. Plus, think about how many variations and combinations of white there are in the world!

At the appointed time, 150 guests attired in white linen congregated on the beach in front of the Dune restaurant at the Ocean Club. All together, we made our way down the stairs from the upper terrace, and onto a path that twisted and wound its way down to the beach. Before stepping onto the white sand, we paused to remove our shoes. And then all the assembled guests gazed straight ahead at the floating mirage before them.

It was like a vision fresh from a romance novel. A gorgeous path, densely strewn with white flower petals, led to an ornate chuppah at the edge of the ocean. The sky was ablaze in color. The wind was blowing. The tide was coming in. The wedding canopy itself was adorned with white organza, which lolled and fluttered and windmilled in the breeze.

As the procession began, haunting, ethereal music by Aria serenaded us from speakers hidden on the beach. It was as though the guests were hearing the wind set to song, as the organza spun and gestured, and the darkening tides touched up against the shore. Every element of the wedding, in fact, was deliberately designed to come alive in the breeze, whether it was the silk streamers that flowed from the bridesmaids' pale rose bouquets, or the chiffon bows decorating the baskets that the flower girls carried.

Now the wedding party appeared. First came fourteen groomsmen and a single groomswoman (Andrew had requested that Karen Lauder, his close friend from childhood days, be "on his side"), all attired in white linen Ralph Lauren shirts and pants. They were

followed by ten bridesmaids in white satin gowns designed by Calypso; then two maids of honor, including one of Andrew's daughters; two flower girls (Andrew's youngest daughter and Sandi's niece); and finally, a ring bearer.

Escorted by her parents, and wearing an ultra-chic Vera Wang ivory chiffon gown, with a halter top and a short train (an outfit inspired by the tangerine chiffon Wang confection that actress Charlize Theron wore at the Academy Awards), Sandi made her entrance. In deference to the beachy simplicity of the setting, we'd arranged for her to wear not a veil or a shawl but a flowing chiffon scarf that we'd attached to the nape of the gown's neck. Apart from her beautiful engagement ring, the only jewelry Sandi wore was a pair of stunning pearl drop earrings designed by her close friend Kara Gaffney.

Andrew and Sandi took their places beneath the chuppah. The *Kaori*'s captain, Martin Lucas, stepped forward, emphasizing in his speech how much Sandi had enriched Andrew's life, and offering the couple a heartfelt blessing. Then Rabbi Judy Lewis began the service. Did Andrew and Sandi agree to be each other's partner, lover, best friend "in the pursuit of four-hundred percent happiness"—and to take on life's challenges together, shoulder to shoulder, as husband and wife?

As the bride and groom placed rings on each other's fingers, and kissed, an unexpected cascade of music diverted our attention to the balcony behind the beach. I'd arranged for fifty gospel singers, all dressed in white robes, to serenade the wedding party with a soaring version of "Oh, Happy Day!," and as they began singing, waiters streamed out onto the beach, bearing trays of fizzy magnum champagne. Toward the end of the beachfront champagne reception, and just as the moon was coming out, the white-robed choir rearranged themselves into a sinuous conga line. Each member held a flickering tiki torch. Imagine: fifty people singing, holding torches, their robes billowing in the wind, gently ushering guests back through the palm trees under moonlight, handing out towels to help guests brush sand off their bare feet and retrieve their shoes, and continuing to serenade us as we made our way back through the formal gardens and into the organza-swagged tent, where a fabulous trio (piano, saxophone, bass) picked up the melody of "Oh, Happy Day!" as if resuming a dream that would never end. By now, all 150 guests had smiles wrapped around their faces two and a half times!

Inside the tent, in keeping with the "Colonial Beach" theme, each of six long tables, dressed in cream satin with a white chiffon overlay trimmed in a white sash, bore the name of a Bahamian town, from Nassau to Gustavia. I wanted to give the impression that we'd borrowed the pick of someone's family vault for the place setting. White china adorned with silver charger plates were paired with silver-rimmed crystal, silver candelabras overflowing with fragrant white roses, chic white pillar candles, and dozens upon dozens of flickering votives. I'd also installed discreet lights underneath every table, which lent an otherworldly glow to a room already bathed in heavenly illumination. Overhead, languorously moving ceiling fans kept the room airy and cool. White chiffon panels camouflaged three sides of the tent, while the remaining wall was a mass of white wooden shutters that opened to reveal . . . but I'm getting ahead of myself.

When I assemble a menu, I like to borrow elements from the personal lives of the honorees. In Andrew and Sandi's case, nothing could have been more fitting than to serve their favorite sake, Kaori—in this case, inside delicate stalks of bamboo. For the meal itself, I'd arranged a simple, elegant "white menu," accompanied by a Domaines Ott. Guests started off with a creamy vichyssoise, with a single tender medallion of lobster meat at the bottom, like buried treasure. This was followed by platters of crispy, crackly mesquite-grilled chicken, roasted garlic, shallots, and asparagus, and the crunchiest, most divine french fries you've ever tasted. One platter made do for every six people, lending an intimate, communal feeling to our feast. We finished up with a drink called Sgroppino: a heady, foamy mixture of vodka, Prosecco, and lemon sorbet, whirred to a froth, and served up in long-stemmed champagne glasses.

After several beautiful toasts (and genial roasts), Andrew stood and thanked God for bringing Sandi into his life, "and making me the happiest man in the universe." When the final toast was clinked and drunk, the white shutters of the back wall parted dramatically to reveal—tucked away all this time!—a second tent, identical in magnificence to the first, though this one was hot, gutsy, devil-red, and totally dance-ready.

Anybody up for a party? The guests streamed into this seductive new enclosure, drawn by the jolt and rhythm of music, heading down the steps and onto a cognac-colored carpet. On the ceiling, taut fabric stretched over an installation of luminescent hidden bulbs made the room glow like a light box. As a personal touch, I'd arranged for the bartender to concoct thirteen different flavors of martini, named for, and in honor of, the thirteen bridesmaids who'd attended Sandi. Among the favorites: Alyson's Aly Kat—light rum, sweet vermouth, and a dash of bitters—and Kate's San Francisco Treat—vodka, plus a splash apiece of cranberry and grapefruit juice. In between dances, sexy ottomans and spacious, squishy cushions positioned outside offered refuge to wandering guests, as did a discreet cigar and cognac bar (both the men and the women indulged).

An all-white extravaganza on a wind-whipped beach, followed by a red-hot one. Foamy Sgroppinos. Beautiful fashions, best friends. Dancing until early morning to everything from "Your Love Is My Love" to "Hot! Hot! Hot!" to *don't-stop* Caribbean tunes. Andrew and Sandi's was a wedding, and a destination weekend, that none of the 150 guests would ever forget. Most everyone agreed that the peak of the night was when Andrew jumped onstage with the band, after hours, to lay down his own drum solo to the Santana tune "Smooth." (As the groom confided jokingly to me later, "You've merchandized me better than anyone has ever done in my life!")

Sometime in the early morning, the new bride and groom stole away from the dance floor. Who could blame them? It was their wedding night, after all. But before the two of them took off, Andrew left us with a farewell gesture by arranging for the hotel to serve the remaining guests one of his favorite guilty pleasures: Philly cheese-steak sandwiches. It was an inventive touch that punctuated a beautiful night, a glorious weekend, friendship, and, of course, long-lasting love.

MENU

VICHYSSOISE WITH LOBSTER MEDALLIONS

KAORI JUNMAI GINGO

∾

FLOWER OF ENDIVE

with Watercress, Frisée, Goat Cheese, and Toasted Pine Nuts

DOMAINES OTT COTES DE PROVENCE BLANC DE BLANC 1977

∾

MESQUITE-GRILLED BABY CHICKEN

with Roasted Garlic and Shallots, Asparagus, and Crispy French Fries

∾

SGROPPINOS

WEDDING CAKE

Ocean

Beach
Ceremony
5:45 p.m.

Pathway to Reception

Pool

Dinner 8 p.m.

To After-party

After-party 10 p.m.

Stage

Bar

Cake

Beds

Cognac and Cigar Bar

A WEDDING WELCOME: IT'S IN THE BAG

Why not arrange to have welcome baskets or goodie bags waiting for your guests when they arrive at their hotel? As a gesture, it's both chic and thoughtful. It tells friends and family members how grateful you are that they've come all this way, and that you've thought ahead about their every comfort and need. Ultimately, it makes your guests feel special, and personally singled out, which is no small feat.

The rattan welcome bags that Andrew and Sandi left in each of their guests' hotel rooms were a wonderful mixture of utility and whimsy that set the tone for the festivities to come. In each basket was a bottle of sunscreen, sarongs for the women, CDs and fragrant candles so that guests could relax in between events, cold bottles of Evian water, and even a roll of quarters for the slot machines at the Ocean Club casino. Best of all was a personal welcome note from the bride and groom, as well as a schedule of the weekend's events.

Does it matter what you put inside a welcome basket? No. It could be simple or elaborate, modestly priced or over-the-top. Let your setting be your guide. If you're getting married in Manhattan, consider arranging for your guests to receive the Sunday *New York Times,* along with some fresh bagels, cream cheese, and a few

slices of Scotch salmon. A package for a ski-resort wedding might include a ski map, fuzzy hand warmers, a beautiful mug, and a packet of hot chocolate for après-ski. Have fun. Be inventive but also practical. Your guests will love you for it.

Along with gifts, notes, and other personal touches, don't forget to include a schedule of what the upcoming wedding weekend will entail: where to go and what time to show up; how to navigate the property, town, or city; the dress code for each event; and who to contact if they find themselves in an unexpected jam. If you know the nights tend to get chilly, recommend that guests bring shawls or sweaters. A well-informed guest is a happy guest.

Finally—and here's a chic touch—consider branding your wedding weekend with your own insignia. Emboss your logo, initials, wedding date, and a copy of your wedding invitation on a tailor-made CD of fabulous tunes, or even a mini-booklet (you can print it out on your home computer) that recounts every up, down, and sideways of your great romance. As time goes by and memories inevitably fade, your guests will have a one-of-a-kind memento of your wedding weekend.

LOVE IN THE TIME OF COLONIAL CHIC

Adi Kabatchnick and Jerry Greenberg

SANTA BARBARA, CALIFORNIA

JULY 8, 2000

The location of a wedding celebration is incredibly important, as Adi Kabatchnick and Jerry Greenberg found out during a far-flung search. We were combing both coasts for the perfect setting when the bride—a smart, modern woman who's never been shy about challenging tradition—blurted out, "Colin, we don't need to look any further! We've fallen in love with a property!" From the moment she laid eyes on the private estate in Santa Barbara, Adi knew: This must be the place.

The setting was even more exotic than she described. Tucked away in a mountainous valley, the grounds resembled a mini Garden of Eden (with a seductive Far Eastern twist). Slender, swaying ferns. A formal rose garden. Cascading waterfalls. Rustic footbridges. Koi ponds stocked with tropical fish—part of a wildlife collection that included ostriches, peacocks, and other exotic, roaming animals. A beautiful main house with a tropical colonial-Indonesian feel, reflected in its red zinc roof and its veranda trimmed with white scalloped wooden detail. The setting complemented Adi and Jerry's tastes to a T.

Adi and Jerry wanted their wedding to be "grand and otherworldly," but at the same time, intimate and cozy. Moreover, as Adi's parents are Israeli, she was eager to incorporate a handful of Jewish traditions into the ceremony and reception. The bride and the groom also both adore Japanese food. The combination of their backgrounds and passions, and our Anglo-Asian setting, created a romantic, cross-cultural extravaganza no one would ever forget.

For our nearly 250 guests, we needed an area that would accommodate the ceremony, reception, and after-party with comfort—and luxury—to spare. I decided to create an elaborate extension of the main house, using its distinctive colonial style and Asian detailing to guide my inspiration. Guests making their way inside the ornate dinner tent would have no idea the structure hadn't been there for years (and I wasn't planning on telling them, either!).

We began assembling our floor plans: We would stage the wedding ceremony almost in the round, underneath a trellised arbor at the entrance to the rose garden. To get there, guests would pass under a matching arbor my team would construct by weaving and entwining the wood with magnificent blooming roses. A short walk away over one of the estate's many foot-

bridges, we would set up round tables dressed in sumptuously embroidered and beaded Indian fabrics to serve as our cocktail area. Large baskets filled with flowering hydrangea and dripping with orchids would be suspended from the trees. Behind the main house, our canopied reception tent would be divided into a trio of dining levels. The top tier would be a terrace stylistically identical to the one enveloping the house and decorated with ornate Oriental rugs on a mahogany-stained wooden floor, colonial wicker furniture, market umbrella—covered round tables, and lush banana trees. The middle level would be the main dining area for the bridal party and family members, anchored with three long, formal tables around the sunken dance floor, with strategically placed round tables scattered into the mix. On the lowest level, lushly overgrown rattan planters with ferns and beautiful exotic blooming orchids would surround the dance floor.

Our stylized Asian garden theme found its way inside our save-the-date cards and invitations. At a gift shop, I stumbled upon a gorgeous intricate silk-screened paper, an intoxicating swirl of lime-green, citrine-yellow, and metallic-gold inks that evoked the smoke and mystery of the Far East. Using this sexy palette, stationer Cindy Loon created a save-the-date card, which she embellished with a white ribbon and a fern-leaf overlay. The wedding invitation was created by lining the back of a heavy-stock cream card with this same beautiful silk-screened paper. Cindy used the paper as a mat beneath a second card (and also to line the envelopes), engraving the wedding details in forest-green ink. After wrapping the cards in lustrous green parchment, she closed them with a bamboo twig and a coin of gold sealing wax.

Guests arriving on Friday found in their hotel rooms elegant, grass-green rattan welcome boxes spilling over with apples, chocolates, a bottle of fine local wine, and a lovely coffee-table book on Santa Barbara. They had plenty of time to relax before that night's rehearsal dinner at the nearby Citronelle restaurant, where they would enjoy fine dining, roasts, and toasts late into the evening.

Then on to the wedding day!

Adi began her morning with a relaxing massage to smooth her knotted nerves (I always tell the bride that something might go wrong at the wedding, but not to give it a second thought, as she's surrounded by professionals who will take care of it). After a stylist and artist completed Adi's hair and makeup, her mother helped her lace up the back of her couture wedding gown—which was truly something to behold.

Romantic and old-world, but also unique and contemporary, Adi's gown was strapless and corseted, with sky-blue, mint, and lilac silk flowers cascading down the sides—a nod to our wedding palette. The material was 100 percent silk radzimir, with a basque waist and pale green stitching around the boning. At the bustle floated a whimsical blue butterfly clasp. Adi's hair, worn down and pulled back by a headband the mint-green stitching of which matched her gown's, was simple and effortlessly chic. Around her neck hung the shimmering diamond necklace that Jerry had given her as a wedding gift twenty-four hours earlier.

Attired in pastel raw-silk dresses, ties, and vests that echoed the exquisite silk flowers on Adi's gown, the bridal party made its way along the rose petal–carpeted, S-shaped aisle that snaked and flowed its way into the garden. Jerry, clad in a cream linen suit and lavender tie, waited with his parents beneath the tall chuppah, which we'd decorated with a seemingly endless garland of lush Virginia and Iceberg roses. As a string quartet began to play Beethoven's "Romance," Adi crossed the bridge and glided down the ethereal path on the arm of her father.

The ceremony, led by Rabbi Philip Aronson, was both tender and joyful. Amidst friends and family members, Jerry and Adi exchanged their vows in English and in Hebrew, and sipped wine from the kiddush cup. Then came a moment of utter enchantment. As Jerry stamped down on a wineglass—a Jewish tradition—and the audience called out, in response, "Mazel tov!," we pulled a cord attached to a trough above the trellis. Hundreds upon hundreds of delicate pink and lavender rose petals tumbled down onto the newlyweds as they embraced. They then made their way back down the aisle, hand in hand, to the strains of Handel's "Arrival of the Queen of Sheba."

The champagne reception floated past as if in a dream. To the delicate rhythms of a jazz trio, guests dined on caviar served on mother-of-pearl spoons; a roasted ratatouille of vegetables filled with goat cheese; fresh shrimp and soft, flaky crab cakes; miniature skewers of lamb; and iced gazpacho served in demitasse cups. For seafood lovers, several raw bars spilled over with fresh lobster, shrimp, oysters on the half shell, cherrystone clams, and crabs. Guests could mix, mingle, and merge, or take seats at round cocktail tables, which I'd dressed in lime green with chic beaded overlays and matching linen napkins, and studded with exotic orchids in Oriental porcelain containers.

Following the reception, guests made their way along the veranda onto a hydrangea-lined flagstone pathway, then up the steps and under the canopy toward the enticing sounds of the L.A.-based band Soulville. The ceiling was swagged in ivory cotton, the tables dressed in a trio of different styles, the carpeting sisal. The bride's and groom's families took seats at long dark colonial wood tables with white place mats, crisp, white embroidered linens, crystal candelabra, and Oriental porcelain jardinieres packed and blooming with locally grown garden roses. The colonial silver was deliberately mismatched, and the glasses came in three sizes, giving the impression that they'd come straight out of the family's collection. Behind the bandstand, which we'd skirted in bamboo, light-filtering wooden shutters concealed our kitchen and service area, throwing an otherworldly glow onto the room, and lending the dreamily glamorous feeling of an era gone by.

For our second style, guests had to look no farther than the dozen round tables situated on the main floor. These were covered first in linen, then topped with sheer, beaded, and embroidered overlays trimmed in luscious bronze ribbon. The flowers, a combination of Leonidas and Sari roses, were clustered into Chinese cachepots. Overhead, ceiling fans sent down a moody, languid breeze.

Finally, the veranda displayed our third style: thirteen round tables underneath market umbrellas, each table dressed with leaf-patterned linens and rattan-and-brass-rimmed chargers. We'd placed Oriental rugs and banana trees on the floor and dotted the tables with

moss-green candles and flowering orchid plants. From the outdoor balcony, guests could glance down on a ravine whose banks were decorated with flickering candlelit trees.

Adi and Jerry's first dance was to Ray Noble's wistfully romantic "The Very Thought of You," a ballad that reflected the couple's love of the music of the 1930s and '40s. But why stop with Ray Noble? What about a little Irving Berlin? With apologies to Fred and Ginger, never has a couple danced as gracefully to "Cheek to Cheek" as Adi and her very proud father. Heaven . . . they were in heaven.

One of the reception's most beautiful moments had its origins in a lovely Jewish tradition: formally crowning a mother with a garland of flowers when her last child is married. In Jerry's case, he was the last of his four siblings to walk down the aisle, and his mother was duly honored.

Our stylish Asian theme continued during dinner. The famed chef Joachim Splichal of Patina Catering prepared hamachi sashimi with Japanese mushrooms, then a salad topped with toasted pecans and Asian pears, followed by a dry-aged sirloin steak with Matsutake mushrooms. As for the wedding cake, it had to be seen (and tasted) to be believed. I designed the cake with Linda Goldsheft. It had five tiers that resembled an intricate bottle-green-and-white Wedgwood china pattern: three of white chocolate cake with white chocolate mousse and raspberries, and two of dark chocolate with the same filling. Linda covered the entire cake with white chocolate Swiss buttercream and green fondant, and white grape leaves and vase detailing with fondant and royal icing, even mimicking the white scallop pattern of the main building's architecture. A true culmination of all the elements.

Typically, after the wedding cake is cut, many guests will slip away into the night. Not these guests! They stayed late, never, ever wanting the enchantment to come to an end.

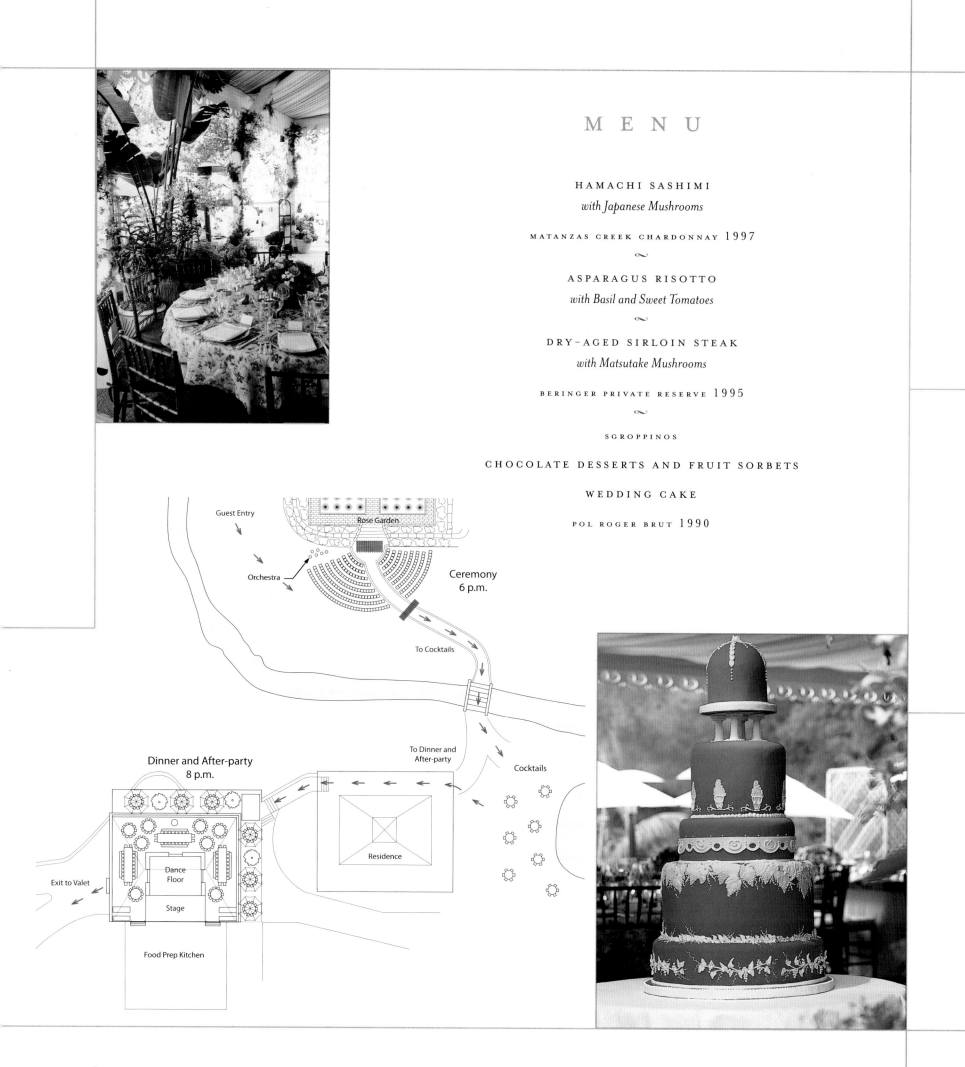

MENU

HAMACHI SASHIMI

with Japanese Mushrooms

MATANZAS CREEK CHARDONNAY 1997

∽

ASPARAGUS RISOTTO

with Basil and Sweet Tomatoes

∽

DRY-AGED SIRLOIN STEAK

with Matsutake Mushrooms

BERINGER PRIVATE RESERVE 1995

∽

SGROPPINOS

CHOCOLATE DESSERTS AND FRUIT SORBETS

WEDDING CAKE

POL ROGER BRUT 1990

Guest Entry

Rose Garden

Orchestra

Ceremony
6 p.m.

To Cocktails

To Dinner and
After-party

Cocktails

Dinner and After-party
8 p.m.

Dance
Floor

Stage

Exit to Valet

Residence

Food Prep Kitchen

Twenty years from now, you don't want to be flipping through your wedding album, murmuring, "Oh my God, what was I thinking?" Your bridal makeup should be classic and timeless; it should never reflect what's considered hot at the time. Don't go with something that's not you just because it's trendy! Wedding makeup should be about enhancing the features nature gave you, and looking luminous and beautiful.

According to Eugenia Weston, of Senna Creations, who did Adi's makeup, a bride should look like herself . . . just a more polished version. A few typical mistakes brides make? According to Weston: "A look that is too dramatic or heavy. Too much blush. Eyeliner that's too thick and too dark. Too much shine and glitter. Obvious lip liner. And blue, green, or overly colorized eye shadows that compete with her features rather than enhance them."

She has a few suggestions (and remedies):

Try out several makeup artists before committing to one. Meet with your artist for a pre-rehearsal one to three months before the wedding, in case you have to audition another. Once you've decided on the right makeup artist, have him or her provide you with a list of products and colors so you can duplicate your "look" easily and precisely.

Carry out a complete "beauty dress rehearsal." Have your hair done the way you'll wear it on your wedding day. Try on your veil and jewelry, along with your wedding-day makeup. Then take pictures and study them carefully. Do all of the elements work well together? Anything you want to change, tweak, discard, enhance? Tell your makeup artist.

Brides are known to shed a few tears—and weddings can last till dawn—so consider products that are both smudge-proof and durable. Weston suggests a waterproof mascara; a cream blush with powder blush applied over it; a moisturizer with SPF in a lightweight or oil-free formula (to prevent sunburn during outdoor pictures); a lipstick sealer; and finally, a light dusting of translucent powder to set the whole look.

Many brides get dressed during the day, and photographers tend to take formal photographs in the late afternoon. In the hours following the ceremony, when the sun has set, the light is an altogether different story—and ambience—which typically calls for more blush and a darker lipstick. Consider keeping your makeup artist on hand so you'll be ready for every conceivable close-up. Or do it yourself by tucking a few "touch-up" products inside your purse, including a pressed-powder compact with puff or brush, concealer and eye cream, lip liner and lipstick, oil-blotting papers, a few cotton swabs, and blush.

IT'S A WONDERFUL TOWN

Julia Power and Edward Weld

NEW YORK CITY

MAY 12, 2002

Julia Power wanted her wedding to be traditional and "ladylike" (in her words), but also stylish and coolly contemporary. While she was eager to honor the spirit of previous generations, she also wanted to spare her guests their more stuffy conventions, from little round tables and dancing during dinner to chicken à-la-something-or-other for four hundred.

What better place for old-fashioned tradition to rub up against present-day chic than New York City, where Julia and her fiancé, Edward Weld, lived and worked? For the wedding ceremony, we chose Manhattan's landmark St. Bartholomew's Church, a soaring, elegant East Side cathedral located on tulip-filled Park Avenue. The reception would take place amidst the 250-acre grounds of the New York Botanical Garden, a setting so idyllic you'd swear you were hundreds of miles from any city (there's a waterfall and river, ponds, a rose and perennial garden, as well as displays of daylilies, orchids, conifers, and flowering trees).

As for dining, Julia confessed to a long-standing love of the *politesse* of the 1940s and '50s: the very best china, fresh flowers everywhere, "and never a bottle of beer in sight after sundown"—the style, in fact, in which her own grandparents once entertained. For that reason and others, Julia was thrilled when we decided for our after-party to re-create the chic, elegant era of New York's glamorous nightclub El Morocco, known to its dazzling clientele (gangsters, movie stars, international high-lifers and civilians alike), as Elmo's. We would decorate the site with red and black lacquer, and the same glamorous zebra-print fabric that once enveloped El Morocco's main salon.

But first things first. For our out-of-town guests, stationer Ellen Weldon created a beautiful save-the-date card, an accordion folder overflowing with suggestions of extravagant, fun things to do in New York City—great restaurants, first-class hotels, and divine shopping recommendations. Julia penciled in a few insider's tips of her own on how to "blend in" with New Yorkers (hint: Don't walk around looking up at the skyscrapers; it's a giveaway). For the church ceremony, Ellen designed elegant programs in ecru stock, with a silver-engraved monogram decorating the cover—a monogram that would adorn every single seating card, printed menu, matchbox, table linen, and chair cover.

When the wedding day came, a lone, celebratory trumpet announced Julia's arrival at St.

Bartholomew's Cathedral. She looked resplendent in a silk organza gown with Alençon lace from Vera Wang, with a matching organza-and-lace shrug. She held an antique purse handle fitted with a new white pouch decorated with her marital monogram. For the eight brides-maids, Shannon McLean of Cose Bella in New York City had designed robin's-egg-blue dresses in zibeline fabric, while bouquets and floral arrangements were created to comple-ment the pale blue hue—luxurious combinations of white Bianca and Vendela roses, white peonies and blue English hydrangeas.

Julia's father, John, escorted his daughter down the candlelit aisle to the altar, where the groom and the Reverend Jay Sidebotham were waiting. The wedding ceremony was deliber-ately low-key, highly personal, and quietly spiritual, mixing readings, blessings, and prayers. It reached an exultant climax when the newlyweds exited the majestic cathedral to a waiting 1960s black Rolls-Royce, and guests showered them with white rose petals. (We even went so far as to tie the traditional JUST MARRIED sign to the Rolls-Royce's back bumper for their ride to the gardens.)

It was time for Act Two! The entrance to the New York Botanical Gardens is just fifteen minutes from the city. Guests streamed through a pair of gorgeous French doors, and then into an arboretum cocktail area, where the walls were blanketed with densely growing ferns. In the center of the room, atop sisal carpeting and surrounded by 1950s-style rattan furni-ture, adorned with roses and votives, sat tables laden with a truly stunning display of seafood.

An hour later, when dinner was announced, guests made their way through a long, cream taffeta–walled hallway, and into a black-and-white-checkered entry foyer. Inside the dining room, they were greeted by three ascending levels of seating arrangements. On the ground floor, center stage amidst the same black-and-white-checkered pattern, stood the bridal party table, a single long twenty-four-foot banquet table with monogrammed slipcovered chairs. One level up stood groupings of round tables. Another level up revealed long ban-quet tables ideal for seating larger groups. A plush, custom-dyed robin's-egg-blue carpet covered each elevated area. Anchoring the room, and holding court over the main table, was an enormous crystal chandelier, which hung down like an intricate display of wintry crystals.

Though the space was large enough to comfortably seat 250 guests, the delicately swagged ceiling and gentle blue-and-silver gelled lighting created an intimate, magic-tinged *Doctor Zhivago*–like feeling. Slender white candles added to the elegance and conviviality of the setting. (You almost expected snowflakes to begin gently falling from the ceiling.) The Todd Londagin Trio supplied the softly evocative supper music, serenading the room with the Gershwin brothers' "Someone to Watch Over Me" as Julia and Edward took their seats.

Julia had requested a menu that was "anything but ordinary." Done! Accompanied by a crisp Killerby Chardonnay, the dinner menu we designed with Glorious Foods began with demitasse cups of rich asparagus soup topped with caviar, followed by a Cavaillon melon filled with a seafood salad in a melon-and-cilantro emulsion. For our main course, guests feasted on a roasted rack of lamb paired with a mélange of vegetables, and a potato tart flecked with truffle shavings.

Family took center stage following the first course, as a movie screen appeared and guests were regaled with scenes from the bride's and groom's childhoods. When the video finished, the screen retracted, and the cool blue lighting gave way to the warmest shades of amber and gold, ideal for dining and great conversation.

Sylvia Weinstock's hazelnut-and-mocha-cream confection was both an extravaganza and a heartfelt family tribute. In addition to the embroidery pattern of piped-in buttercream, and the hand-molded blue and white sugar flowers, Sylvia had created a trio of special symbols out of marzipan: two bumblebees and a dragonfly, in honor of three late, and greatly missed, family members. At the base of the cake were eight miniature satellite fruitcakes, soaked in fine rum and cognac, and baked by Julia's mother, who'd also sent Sylvia a crate of Meyer lemons from the family's Palm Desert, California, orchard so that the cake designer could create a lemon-curd filling for several of the layers.

After the cake was cut, a set of draperies opened . . . and it was time for Act Three! Welcome to the millennium version of New York's fabled night spot El Morocco! The chic glass-top-tabled, patent-leathered, zebra-striped room, with its blazing red couches and ink-black ottomans, was revealed in all its opulence, and guests were agog—especially when the band, Soulville, who'd flown in specially from Los Angeles, kicked up their first number. To mark the after-party's change in mood, atmosphere, and emotional temperature, Julia had changed into dance-floor-friendly attire—a white dupioni silk strapless dress that Shannon McLean had created for her to wear not long before to the Metropolitan Museum of Art's Costume Institute gala honoring Jacqueline Kennedy's White House years.

Julia and Edward's first dance was to Sting's version of George and Ira Gershwin's "My One and Only," an untraditional choice that nonetheless had strong meaning for the couple. Julia had once heard the singer perform the song live at a private party. At that moment, after fifteen years spent living in Los Angeles, "I decided I would move to New York. It was the best decision I have ever made"—in large part, she confessed, because she met Edward a month later.

The hours ticked past in a sexy, glamorous blur of dancing, socializing, and celebrating. One A.M. Two A.M. Three A.M. Why stop? No one wanted to leave the party—even with the added incentive of wonderful parting gifts, including homemade fruitcake, and a special package from candy company Harbour Sweets of Massachusetts, in honor of Edward's late father and his love of Cape Cod (Ellen Weldon had created paper sailboats trimmed in pale silver to house the shell- and starfish-shaped candies).

Determined to bid all their guests farewell, the newlyweds were the last to leave. "We weren't sorry," said Julia in retrospect, "until we missed our flight to Hawaii that morning. Well, it was worth it."

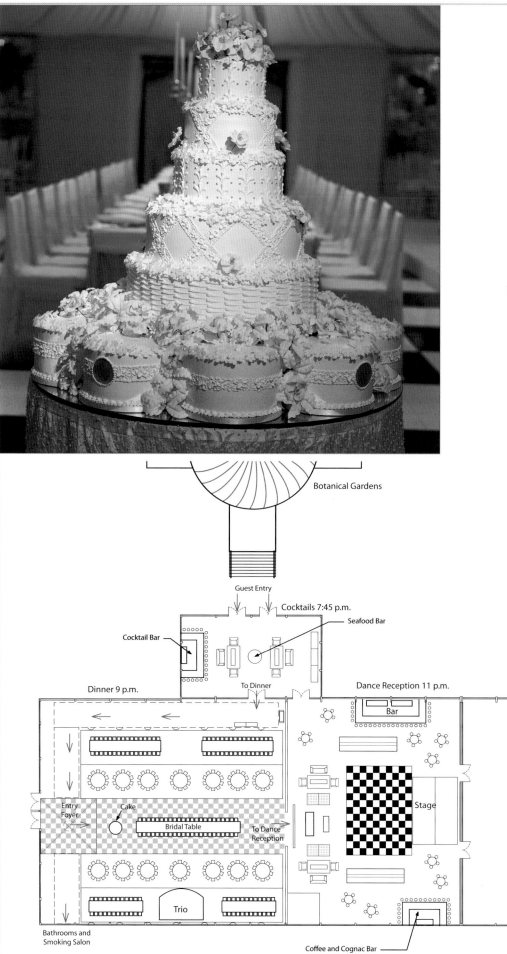

Botanical Gardens

Guest Entry

Cocktails 7:45 p.m.

Seafood Bar

Cocktail Bar

Dinner 9 p.m.

To Dinner

Dance Reception 11 p.m.

Bar

Entry Foyer

Cake

Bridal Table

To Dance Reception

Stage

Trio

Bathrooms and Smoking Salon

Coffee and Cognac Bar

MENU

ASPARAGUS SOUP

CAVIAR AND CRÈME FRAÎCHE

❧

CAVAILLON MELON NEPTUNE

with Lobster, Scallops, and Red Snapper

KILLERBY CHARDONNAY 1998

❧

ROASTED RACK OF SPRING LAMB

with Sauce Romarin

MÉLANGE OF HARICOTS VERTS,

BABY CARROTS, FAVA BEANS,

Artichoke Hearts, and Fresh Morels

POTATO TART

with Shaved Truffles

IMPERIAL RESERVA RIOJA 1994

❧

FROZEN STRAWBERRY SOUFFLÉ

with Rhubarb Compote

❧

WEDDING CAKE

DEMITASSE

BOLLINGER BRUT

THE MANE EVENT: YOUR WEDDING HAIR

The late, legendary Madison Avenue stylist John Sahag created an elegant upsweep for Julia Power—"reminiscent of Princess Grace; very elegant and regal, with a lot of attention to detail in the back." For Sahag, creating a hairstyle was all about theater, about creating "a character that fits within the wedding story," creating a modern hairstyle "with a slight edge to it." He liked to point out that a typical (though understandable) mistake many brides make is to adopt an outdated hairstyle from their mother's generation.

For brides, a coif consultation and preliminary tryout are a must, at least two months before the wedding. "It's incredibly important to meet with a stylist and communicate the look you want—maybe even bring a few photos from magazines," advised Sahag. "Bring photos of your wedding dress—bodice, neckline, back, and train. Also explain exactly what your headpiece will look like—a tiara, headband, wreath of flowers, etc.—and if possible bring it with you. Your hairstyle is an accessory as well—it should always complement, never detract from, your gown."

Following the "tryout," take pictures of the finished style from every angle so you can study them at home. Sahag suggested, "Look them over carefully and consider, 'Is this exactly what I want? Or could we make some small adjustments? Softer sides? More or less wave? A touch of highlights around the hairline?'" This isn't the time to be shy—tell your stylist.

You might also consider asking your stylist to be on-site to help you remove the veil after the ceremony. Often, an elaborate headpiece or veil weighs a bride's hair down, and when she removes it, the style is destroyed. "A stylist can quickly retouch and restore it," said Sahag.

Bottom line: A bride should be 100 percent happy and 100 percent confident that her hair will look nothing less than gorgeous throughout her wedding day.

FIRE AND ICE ON THE MOUNTAIN

Deborah Guerrera and Casey Cowell

BEAVER CREEK, COLORADO

MARCH 14, 1999

The elegant, secluded ski resort of Beaver Creek, Colorado, had been a vacation home for Deborah Guerrera and Casey Cowell for years, and they'd just put the finishing touches on a penthouse condo with jaw-dropping mountain views. So it came as no surprise when they told me that they fantasized about taking their wedding vows atop one of the area's beautiful snow-covered peaks.

Deb and Casey are casual and unpretentious, utterly at home in jeans and T-shirts. They are also famously generous hosts. My challenge was to highlight their personalities by creating a wedding that was both dramatic and romantic—with a dollop of silky grandeur—and also easy, relaxed, and down-to-earth. Deb concurred that we should "go all out," adding, "Halfway to wonderful is never enough." (Ain't *that* the truth!)

Our inspiration, quite naturally, was the mountains . . . and then I took a peek inside Deb's closet. Cranberry everywhere! She adored the color, owned countless outfits in rich ruby shades, and wondered aloud: Could she possibly wear a crimson-colored wedding gown? "Why not?" I answered. When New York–based designer Bob Evans responded by coming up with a magnificent strapless Duchess Satin gown in cranberry with a matching veil and wrap, Deb and I were both enthralled by the primal contrast of red against the white snow. I immediately rushed Deb to the famed furrier Dennis Basso for a full-length sable coat trimmed in the same crimson silk. Out of these elements, our wedding theme was hatched: fire and ice.

This sexy motif would resonate in the cranberry-bordered, cream-colored textured stock that designer Marc Friedland used for our save-the-date cards, wedding invitations, confirmation packages, luggage tags, menus, and place cards. In further homage to our exquisite Colorado backdrop, Mark used an evergreen ink, with a lustrous, matching silk green ribbon as a finishing touch.

On Thursday of the wedding weekend, 140 friends and family members boarded a chartered plane in Chicago and arrived in nearby Vail, where they were whisked away to the Hyatt Regency Beaver Creek. "The weekend should feel like a holiday for everyone," Deb had told me. To that end, guests happily surrendered to their hosts' extraordinary

generosity: welcome boxes in each room, spilling over with chocolate, potpourri, and fragrant candles—not to mention a twenty-four-hour hospitality suite continuously stocked with champagne, wine, cookies, soda, hot chocolate, crudités, afternoon tea, and other goodies; a private concierge; an activities director; ski instructors; and even a portrait artist on call throughout the weekend to capture each guest's (beaming) profile.

Along with all their other accomplishments, Deb and Casey are both excellent swing dancers, so on Friday evening, guests congregated in the hotel for a completely over-the-top "Swinging Soiree." My team had transformed the hotel's ballroom into a chic 1940s fantasy that would have made Bugsy Malone swoon. A cool-cat black-and-white-checkerboard floor. An elevated living room. The chicest, plushest velvet backdrops. Gleaming mirrored tables. Leopard-spot linens. Billiards. Cigars. The men looked slick in zoot suits, fedoras, and spats, while the women were knockouts in 1940s fashions and hairdos. After spinning, twirling, diving, whipping, shagging, jiving, Lindy-ing, jitterbugging, and general vogue-ing, guests dove into a tower of jumbo shrimp, warm creamed asparagus in espresso cups, and a delectable buffet of rack of lamb, assorted cheeses, and over-the-top decadent desserts displayed on a tiered table with a gold urn centerpiece overflowing with black grapes. The legendary swing band the Royal Crown Review kept the place jumping until midnight, when a deejay took over because no one could bear to call it a night!

Later, when guests returned to their hotel rooms, they found a personalized cranberry velvet shoe bag, along with instructions to place the shoes they were planning to wear to the wedding in the bag, and hang it on the door for an early-morning pickup. Why? Because everyone would be using snow boots to get up the mountain!

The next day was a do-as-you-please "free day." The hotel concierge arranged for guests to go skiing, snowmobiling, hot-air ballooning, ice skating—or to simply enjoy head-to-toe pampering with a massage or spa treatment. It was the perfect warm-up for that evening's fairy-tale grandeur.

At five in the afternoon, resplendent in their wedding attire, everyone gathered by the open-air fire pit at the mountainside entrance to the hotel. Something daring and wondrous was about to happen. One by one, guests boarded a procession of open-air sleighs pulled by Sno-Cats and furnished with warm blankets and wraps to keep everybody snug and comfortable, not to mention exhilarated. Braving high snow and icy temperatures, we wound and twisted our way through deep pine and aspen forests to Beaver Creek Mountain, and from

there, headed up another few thousand feet until we reached Beano's Cabin—a fabulous restaurant/private club (and literally, an old-fashioned log cabin) nestled in a vast meadow, shouldered by the dark-white silhouette of Grouse Mountain, which was densely covered with thousands of Aspen trees. Alighting into deep, powdery snow, all 140 guests made their way into a white-canopied tent, past two tall, shapely, intricately ice-sculpted urns posted at the entrance, each spilling over with lush red tulips. We'd arrived!

First, it was time for guests to change out of their snow boots and into their already-warmed evening shoes. Next, we made our way along a spacious, dreamlike corridor. The walls were swagged with cream silk, the richly draped ceiling was adorned with candelabras, and on each side of the corridor, a doughnut of red roses and berries surrounded hurricane candles elevated on tall metal stands. Now all the guests found themselves standing before a table covered with individual leaf-wrapped tapers, one for each guest to carry into the cere-mony tent—but not before they signed and witnessed the oversized marriage certificate, and dropped a wish into a beribboned box that we later presented to the newlyweds.

Our candles lit, we took our seats in the ceremony tent, and waited there.

No one was prepared for the almost mythic glamour of Deb's entrance. It was as though we were all kids again, and inside a fantastical fairy tale. After pulling up solo in a horse-drawn sleigh the color of crimson berries, Deb alit, a magical mirage wrapped in sable from head to toe over her cranberry-red gown, a choker of sparkling diamonds around her throat. Before she came down the aisle, she removed the sable coat, and the vision of cranberry against the winter-white was breathtaking. Through an ocean of candlelight, Deb slowly made her way down the aisle to the altar overlooking the mountain, where she met up with the handsome groom. A lavish, oversized wreath of red roses over both their heads appeared to halo the couple. But where were the groomsmen, the bridesmaids, the flower girls, the

best man, the minister? There were none. Adding to the fairy-tale glamour of our evening, Casey and Deb were permitted by Colorado law to marry themselves, the only requirement being the presence of two witnesses. (Two? There were 140 of us!)

Yet the bride and groom weren't by themselves at the altar. By their sides stood the five children they were bringing to their marriage. Deb explained to the assembled guests that she wanted their children to be front and center at the ceremony, since all of them were joining to create a wonderful new family, and a wonderful new life.

The ceremony was a visual and emotional feast, beautiful and romantic. For their vows, Deb and Casey had written simple love letters to each other. As they pronounced themselves man and wife, large oil drums outside in the snow burst into primitive, exultant flames, sending wild shadows and patterns over the snow. Moments later, we started to illuminate the entire mountain around us with theatrical lighting. It was truly, profoundly spectacular.

To celebrate, we drank countless magnums of vintage Dom Pérignon.

Afterward, guests crowded into the dining room, where they were met with a hot, roaring fireplace, rustic overhead chandeliers made of curving antlers, and a sumptuous array of food stations, each bearing serving vessels and platters custom-carved out of shimmering rock crystal–like ice. We had paired the food and drinks. What's your mood? Imperial Beluga caviar and Dom Pérignon vintage champagne? Scottish smoked salmon and cured gravlax with frozen infused vodka? Stone crab claws with Joe's Famous Mustard Sauce (specially flown in from Miami) alongside an ice-cold Meursault? And for a main course, what about mouthwatering roasted veal loin with mushrooms, and filet mignon cooked to perfection and hand-sliced to order in a delicious Bordelaise sauce, both complemented by a superb Bordeaux?

Since fire and ice—and fairy tales—couldn't be improved upon, the tables were dressed simply: a creamy pin-dot linen topped with an overcloth of rusty brown suede, and adorned with countless centerpieces of cranberry and deep-red roses. Outside, the tall trees, like a second tier of spectators, were illuminated with hundreds of bulbs, creating an enchanted forest of light for guests to gaze out at as they dined.

As for the wedding cake, the magicianly Polly Schoonmaker outdid herself. It *looked* as if she'd hand-pressed colorful, luscious rose hips, cranberries, and hawthorn berries onto

each of the four tiers—but her handwork was far more detailed (and dazzling) than that. She had created the berries out of red marzipan, deepened and enhanced their color with beet powder dust, and used dark chocolate for the leaves and delicate stems. Polly picked up our wedding colors—buckskin, cream, and cranberry—within an eggshell cream base of fondant, which she'd laid atop a buttercream-iced chocolate-mousse layer cake. On the surface of each tier was another round of fondant, and Polly had added a flourish to each tier's upper edge with a sleek fondant ribbon of the deepest, darkest cranberry. On alternating tiers, she also replicated the wonderfully rough-hewn texture of our linens by sponging on the texture with parchment paper dipped in a loose royal icing.

For the cutting of the cake, guests made their way back inside the ceremony tent. Except . . . it was no longer a wedding tent. We'd transformed it into an over-the-top sexy nightclub, complete with a dance floor that all but shouted out, *C'mon!* Amidst riotous dancing, guests toasted Deb and Casey with Taittinger Comtes de Champagne Rosé, the only question being: Who would last longer—the band or the by-now-delirious guests? Sometime after one A.M., the band proved the unofficial winners. Guests then found their way out onto the deck for congratulatory cigars, cognac, and to-die-for champagne truffles. After a quick trip down the mountain, guests found "hangover remedy" packs on their pillows to ensure that they would be ready for one more soiree the next day: an informal farewell brunch hosted by Deb and Casey in their mountain-facing penthouse. "I think by the end of the weekend, everyone—even if they had been strangers before—was family, and felt at home," Deb said. "Of everything from that wonderful weekend, this is what I will cherish the most."

MENU

IMPERIAL BELUGA CAVIAR STATION

with Traditional Accompaniments (Egg Whites and Yolks, Melba Toast, Lemon Wedges, and Crème Fraîche)

MAGNUMS OF DOM PÉRIGNON VINTAGE CHAMPAGNE

∾

SCOTTISH SMOKED SALMON AND CURED GRAVLAX

(Served with Russian and Dark Rye Bread)

FROZEN INFUSED VODKAS; FROZEN AQUAVIT

∾

MEDALLIONS OF FOIE GRAS ON ROUNDS OF BRIOCHE

with Cherry Chutney and Apple Slices

COMTES LAFON PERRICRES MEURSAULT 1996 OR CHÂTEAU D'YQUEM SAUTERNES 1990

∾

STONE CRAB STATION

with Joe's Famous Mustard Sauce

ROASTED VEAL LOIN

with Mushrooms and Roasted Filet Mignon with Bordelaise Sauce and Caramelized Onions

SMALL BRIOCHE ROLLS WITH POMMES SOUFFLÉES

CHÂTEAU CHEVAL BLANC ST. EMILION 1990

∾

A SELECTION OF IMPORTED FRENCH CHEESES

(Triple Crème, Bleu, and Chèvre) with Crusty Sourdough Bread, Fresh Figs, and Champagne Grapes

VINTAGE PORT

∾

WEDDING CAKE

with a Blackberry Coulis

TAITTINGER COMTES DE CHAMPAGNE ROSÉ 1990

OR VEUVE CLICQUOT DEMI-SEC NV

∾

TEUSCHER CHAMPAGNE TRUFFLES AND COFFEE

HINE TRIOMPHE AND LOUIS XIV COGNAC

CIGARS

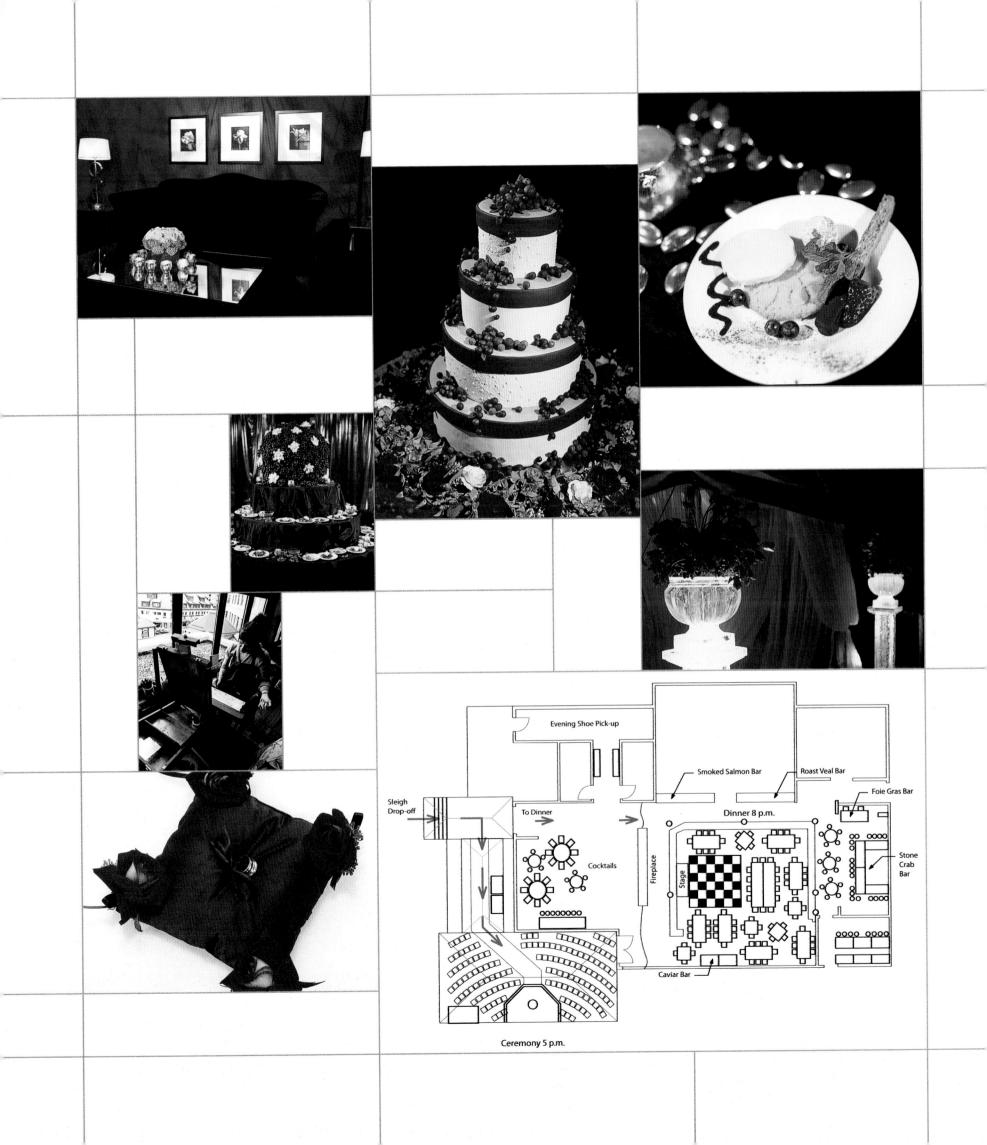

Evening Shoe Pick-up

Smoked Salmon Bar

Roast Veal Bar

Foie Gras Bar

Sleigh Drop-off

To Dinner

Dinner 8 p.m.

Cocktails

Fireplace

Stage

Stone Crab Bar

Caviar Bar

Ceremony 5 p.m.

BEYOND THE WOMAN IN WHITE: CHOOSING YOUR GOWN

There's no rule that says a wedding dress has to be white. Choose your favorite color or a flattering silhouette. As long as you're not offending anyone, follow what your sense of caprice dictates.

Bob Evans, who designed Deb's dress, has a few suggestions:

If red is too avant-garde for your taste, why not go for a soft pastel hue, such as mint green, blush pink, or ice blue? "The effect is beautiful, very Grace Kelly, and just a slight variation on the traditional."

Embroider a simple white gown with intriguing, unexpected details. "It makes it completely unique and special," says Evans. Example: He recently added whimsical butterflies, dragonflies, and hummingbirds to a client's bridal train.

Go for a sleek, sexy shape (not every bride has to resemble Cinderella at the ball). "Most clients come to me asking for a figure-conscious strapless gown or an A-line. The big-skirted look is not that 'in' anymore. You can be a bit more modern these days—sexy and sophisticated is perfectly acceptable."

Top off your outfit with a coat, a shawl, a shrug, even a fur stole. "I've done a white ermine jacket for a winter wedding. I've also known women to do white mink coats over their gowns. It's functional as well as beautiful."

Communicate with your designer or salesperson. "Don't be afraid to speak up if you have ideas. Brides often come to me and say, 'I want to look like Audrey Hepburn' or 'I love "forties fashions."' This helps me understand exactly what mood they want to create when walking down the aisle. My goal is to help each bride realize her fantasy."

A NIGHT AT THE OPERA . . . AND A DAY IN THE GARDEN

NEW YORK CITY

June 24, 1999

GREENWICH, CONNECTICUT

June 27, 1999

Thanks to my close friendship with a bride whose family had a long-standing relationship with New York City's Metropolitan Opera House, I was able to create the very first (and, I have to believe, the very last) private party ever to be held on its legendary stage. From the night of this extraordinary, one-of-a-kind party to the actual wedding day three days later, it was seventy-two hours of magic, elegance, glamour, grandeur, incredible food, opulent costumes, and even (I couldn't resist) live monkeys.

How much fun was it to work at the Met? Frankly, I felt like a kid in a candy store. Certain opportunities come along only once in a lifetime, and without a doubt, this was one of them. The building itself is marvelous. The walls, ceilings, and sets can rise . . . and fall . . . and soar upward again. I could re-create any opera, any scene, any era, any mood, any fantasy. Not to mention the sheer weight of musical history in the air: Callas, Price, Sutherland, Domingo, and Pavarotti, just for starters. Plus, who wouldn't be beside himself to work with the Met's wizardly team of lighting directors and set designers?

The bride and groom are both sophisticated, worldly people who are the life, heart, and soul of any social event lucky enough to have them. I also consider them now to be my closest friends. When we first sat down together, their vision for the evening was relatively modest: They would pick out a menu for their guests, then sit down for dinner on the stage of the Met. Fair enough. But why stop there, I asked? Why not *start* there? Why not create for their friends my very own three-act dinner opera?

Immediately, my mind conjured up images of a black-and-white nineteenth-century ball, the women in luminous ball gowns, the men in white tie. I took out a sketch pad. I drew a single feather. My imagination was in free flight. Because this would be the only time in history the Met permitted such a function on its stage, the three of us agreed to transform the evening into a once-in-a-lifetime soiree. And so I continued sketching, scheming, and dreaming.

Our backdrop? The opulent villa scene from *Der Rosenkavalier,* Richard Strauss's 130-year-old comic opera whose plot involves trysts, sexual intrigue, and, of course, marriage. For my palette, I decided to use black and white, combined with red and Schiaparelli pink, in

homage to Elsa Schiaparelli, the witty, elegant grand dame of fashion designers. Feathers would play an integral part in the festivities (to me, they've always had a very nineteenth-century operatic feel). Also, I've had a lifelong fascination with blackamoors—those stern, beautiful African heads that adorn medieval heraldry—and what more perfect setting to bring these iconic images alive than on one of the most famous opera stages on earth.

Befitting the palette, our invitation was a black-and-white extravaganza, its oversized scale hinting at the larger-than-life enticements that lay ahead. When guests opened it up, their eyes were drawn to two tall, slender, whimsical monkeys propping up the invitation itself, which was inscribed in flouncy, jet-black Jean Cocteau–style handwriting.

The regrets were few and far between. Who in the world would pass up the opportunity to attend a private party on the stage of the Metropolitan Opera House?

Decked out in flashing jewels, stunning gowns, and elegant white tie, our four hundred guests made their way to the Met's upstairs lobby. There, they were met with sumptuous red sofas, shocking pink cushions, and enormous arrangements of red and pink flowers. Following a lavish cocktail reception, it was time for the evening's first (but hardly last) surprise. Enter the blackamoors!

There were ten of them in all, clad in turbans, feathers, and pantaloons, charged with escorting our guests into the auditorium, down the long aisles, and to the base of the legendary Metropolitan stage. There, footmen intercepted the guests and assisted them onto the stage. As soon as the attendees caught sight of *Der Rosenkavalier*'s wildly colorful, gilded ballroom scene—complete with glazed windows, window boxes, and a baroque ceiling looming over red lacquer floors—they were understandably beside themselves.

Onstage, I'd created an elegant pattern of long and round tables. I'd dressed the three long banquet tables in black crinoline petticoats, before covering them with a black-and-white-striped fabric, which permitted the sexiest hint—a *flirtation,* really—of jet-black petticoat to wink out from underneath. Each table was adorned with an overlay of Schiaparelli pink satin, and fringed with four inches of lush, ticklish Austrian crystal beading, and finally . . . a gilded, mirrored tabletop. Every one of our round tables featured an extravagant centerpiece: a pudding of three hundred Jacaranda roses, supported by an underlying cuff of red roses. A delicate cone of pink peonies perched on a gold armature, topped with extravagant plumes of pink ostrich feathers. Both a red glass Tiffany charger and a red water goblet punctuated each place setting, alongside both silver flatware for our dinner courses

and gold flatware for our dessert course (which the bride had made at home). Our napkins were monogrammed Schiaparelli-pink satin, lined in red linen, each bearing a single stitched ruby bead hanging at forty-five degrees at the edge of the plate. Naturally, there were feathers everywhere. In fact, I doubt there was a feather left within a one-hundred-mile radius of New York City!

Once the guests had taken their seats, a hush settled over them. Then a single celestial voice broke the silence. It belonged to the beautiful French soprano Emma Shapplin, and the song was "Cara Mio." At the same time, four twenty-foot chandeliers began to descend, inch by luxurious inch, from the ceiling. Each one was dressed in red velvet, with four feet of silky black tassel on the bottom, and an opulent fan of ostrich feathers above. Simultaneously, the blackamoors reentered the stage, followed by an army of waiters, one per guest, each holding a plate concealed by a sterling silver cloche. On cue, as one, they lifted their cloches. Dinner!

And what a dinner! A caviar tart to begin, followed by a luscious, herbed rack of lamb. For dessert, master confectioner Sylvia Weinstock had created ten different elaborate designs of miniature wedding cakes, all complementing our wedding palette of black and white, red and pink. As dinner wound down, guests were again serenaded, this time by the exquisite voices of the Metropolitan Opera Youth Group. Finally, as the very last note rang out, the ten blackamoors took their places against *Der Rosenkavalier*'s ornate backdrop, and then, as everybody looked on, they opened a set of doors to reveal . . .

. . . *Die Fledermaus*! We'd not only transformed the mood, and the set, we'd changed operas! Welcome to the garden scene from Johann Strauss's celebrated opera—a six-thousand-square-foot playground scored by the sounds of "La Fantasia Espanola" played by the twenty-one-member Sammy Goz Orchestra, whom we'd flown in specially from Paris. Guests, by now happily dazed, wandered into a nineteenth-century dream, complete with a shimmering glass arboretum. To the sides, we'd created sexy, subtly elevated lounges with thick black shag carpet, black patent-leather chairs, mirrored tabletops, and zebra-skin loungelike ottomans, while thick garlands of red anthurium snaked their way around black bamboo columns crowned with palm fronds. Our centerpiece was a wraparound black patent-leather mirror-topped bar, and a huge Chinese pagoda-style cage filled with (I told you!) live, chattering monkeys.

As guests sipped from slender vials of vodka, mint, and lime juice, blended to a froth (along with martinis and magnums of Cru champagne), they gazed down at the waterfall of Austrian-style desserts and what seemed like miles of petits fours—while, thanks to projections, they were entertained by countless images of swinging monkeys.

No one wanted to leave. But all great shows must come to an end. Besides, this was only the beginning of our wedding weekend—and for me, another opportunity to create another custom-crafted dreamscape.

Our festivities took place three days later at the bride's ancestral home on the Connecticut shore. Inside the enormous series of white tents overlooking Long Island Sound, using a palette of mint green, I created a lush, vine-filled, overgrown, elegantly unkempt English potting-shed atmosphere—a lusciously organic tangle of potting barns, ancient terra-cotta pots, oozing mosses, lattices, trellises, sheds, fish-filled fountains, and wildlife. There was hanging moss and wheatgrass mixed in garden boxes spilling over with white blooming orchid plants, and even a four-thousand-square-foot stone floor with matching fountain, which took twenty-one workers approximately three weeks to install. Not to mention a courtyard that I'd filled with vintage birdcages (and yes, they were all occupied).

My aim, as always, is to appeal to all the senses. Inside the tent, guests were met by the fragrance of fresh flowers and musky-sweet soil; they heard the gurgling of fountains; felt the

cool air-conditioned air against their skin; were regaled by the chirps, tweets, and twitterings of birds. If guests closed their eyes, they could believe they were at a lush English estate in Surrey, or Dorset, or Cornwall.

At noon, the highly acclaimed orchestra Orpheus played Handel's "Water Music" as guests entered the ceremony tent and took their seats in snow-white rows of seating divided by garden boxes overflowing with white astilbi. Next came the cantor, the groom and his best man, and the parents of the soon-to-be-newlyweds, followed by the bridal procession and the maid of honor. Finally, to the soaring, multi-voiced grandeur of Lohengrin's "Wedding March," the beautiful bride made her stunning entrance on the arm of her father.

When the ceremony ended, it was time to celebrate. Guests were invited into the cocktail tent, where waiters greeted them with champagne and Beluga caviar passed out on mother-of-pearl spoons. After the champagne reception, the adjacent luncheon tents were revealed, where guests enjoyed a chic trio of tray-passed soups: a gazpacho with confetti vegetable garnish; a chilled curried summer squash with sour cream and chervil; and a chilled asparagus cream garnished with shaved white truffles and truffle oil—Gaelic leaf. Our waiters then passed trays of hand-crafted endive petal bundles. How could something so simple be so incomparably dramatic? The outside of each bundle was six mint-green endive leaves tied together with a leek ribbon. Inside each was a mixture of mesclun, watercress, frisée, and chèvre, drizzled with Dijon vinaigrette. On cue, waiters came around and clipped the ribbons, and the endives, released, opened out, as if kissed by the sun itself.

Shortly thereafter, the guests made their way to the buffet tables, which were abundantly adorned with grill-seared yellowfin tuna with a peppercorn crust; plummy soba noodles; fresh white asparagus; sea bass medallions with rosemary aioli; and a stunning array of smoked and cured fish, from trout and sturgeon to gin-cured citrus salmon.

No one had ever seen a cake as gorgeous as the one Oregon-based cake-maker Polly Schoonmaker concocted. It was three tiers high, and each one of its dark red petals was comprised of three perfect pieces of icing, painstakingly conjoined by hand, jigsaw puzzle–like, to create the icing fabric, a feat that took approximately an hour per inch. The weather was not cooperating, and the cake was melting fast, which encouraged us to invite guests onto the back patio for the cake-cutting, and the groom's heartfelt speech.

After the cake-cutting, we proceeded with the eighteenth-century ritual known as "afternoon tea." It was a bright, breezy afternoon. The water on Long Island Sound snapped and crested. We served perfect miniature sandwiches: watercress and egg; cucumber rounds with an herbed cream cheese; plum tomatoes with fresh basil mayonnaise; and thinly sliced radishes with sweet parsley butter. Not to mention scones, crumpets, madeleines, butter and nut cookies, and, as a chic climax, miniature fresh fruit-shaped sorbets.

What had happened to my friends? The groom, an unapologetic romantic by nature, had chartered a 140-foot yacht, which was anchored a little offshore. The remaining guests made their way to the family dock to bid farewell to the newlyweds as they disappeared inside the boat, motored back to the city, and the very next morning, boarded the Concorde to Europe for a six-week honeymoon. We had become such good friends that I ended up having daily phone calls with the bride and groom while they were on their honeymoon.

MENU

TRAY PASSED APPETIZERS AND SMALL PLATES

Beluga Caviar on Pearl Spoons

Chilled Classic Gazpacho with Confetti Vegetable Garnish

Chilled Curried Summer Squash with Sour Cream and Chervil

Chilled Asparagus Soup with Shaved White Truffle and Truffle Oil—Gaelic Leaf Garnish

*Summer Ragout of North Atlantic Halibut and Scotch Salmon in a Light Nage
of Leeks and Mushrooms on Saffron-Scented Couscous with Parsley Leaf Garnish*

*Endive Petal Bundles, Tied with Leek Ribbons and Filled with Summer Mesclun Greens,
Watercress, Frisée, and Chèvre in Dijon Vinaigrette*

*Mille-feuille of Salmon (Thin Layers of Phyllo Pastry with Smoked Salmon and Imported Caviar
with Whipped Sour Cream and Chive Sauce)*

*Truffled Ravioli, Cabbage/Artichoke Ravioli, and Roasted-Beet Ravioli
with Grilled Artichoke Hearts in Brown Butter*

*Grill-Seared Loin of Yellowfin Tuna
with a Peppercorn Crust, Sliced Rare and with Wasabi Mustard Cream*

BUFFETS

*Soba Noodles in a Light Plum Dressing
with Cashews, Red Pepper, Slivered Snow Peas, Scallions, and Toasted Black Sesame Seeds*

Shredded Asian Lettuces, Baby Corn, and Mustard Green Slaw in a Shallot Sesame Vinaigrette

Tomato Lasagna with Fresh Mozzarella and Parmesan

Vegetable-Stuffed Zucchini with Savory Bread Crumbs

*A Variety of Chilled Asparagus,
including French White Asparagus and Pencil Asparagus, with Walnut Vinaigrette*

Grilled Branzino (Sea Bass) Medallions in an Herb Marinade with Rosemary Aioli

Patatini Potatoes and Garlicky Spinach

Arugula Salad with Olive Oil Dressing and Shaved Parmesan

*Smoked and Cured Fish:
Smoked Trout, Smoked Sturgeon, Smoked Tuna, Gravlax, Pastrami-Cured Salmon, and our own
Gin-Cured Citrus Salmon; served with Dill Mustard Sauce, Wasabi Cream, Red Onion Confit, Capers,
Tomato, Red Onion, and Fresh Lemon*

Fresh Cucumber Salad with Dill Vinaigrette

❧

LOUIS JADOT POUILLY-FUISSÉ 1997

CHÂTEAU DE BEAUCASTEL CHÂTEAUNEUF-DU-PAPE 1996

WEDDING CAKE

TAITTINGER RESERVE 1991

AFTERNOON TEA

TEA SANDWICHES

*Watercress and Egg; Thinly Sliced Radishes with
Sweet Parsley Butter; Plum Tomatoes with
Fresh Basil Mayonnaise; Cucumber Rounds with
Herbed Cream Cheese;
Smoked Salmon Pinwheels and Albacore Tuna and Herb
Mayonnaise*

SCONES, CRUMPETS, AND MADELEINES
with Clotted Cream

INDIVIDUAL DARK CHOCOLATE MOUSSE
IN CHOCOLATE PASTRY CUPS

WHITE CHOCOLATE CHEESECAKE
SOUFFLÉ TART
on a Graham Cracker Crust with Fresh Raspberries

AN ASSORTMENT OF DELICATE WAFER,
BUTTER, AND NUT COOKIES,
*Fresh Berry Tarts with Burnt-Butter Custard,
and Espresso and Citrus Rind Shortbread*

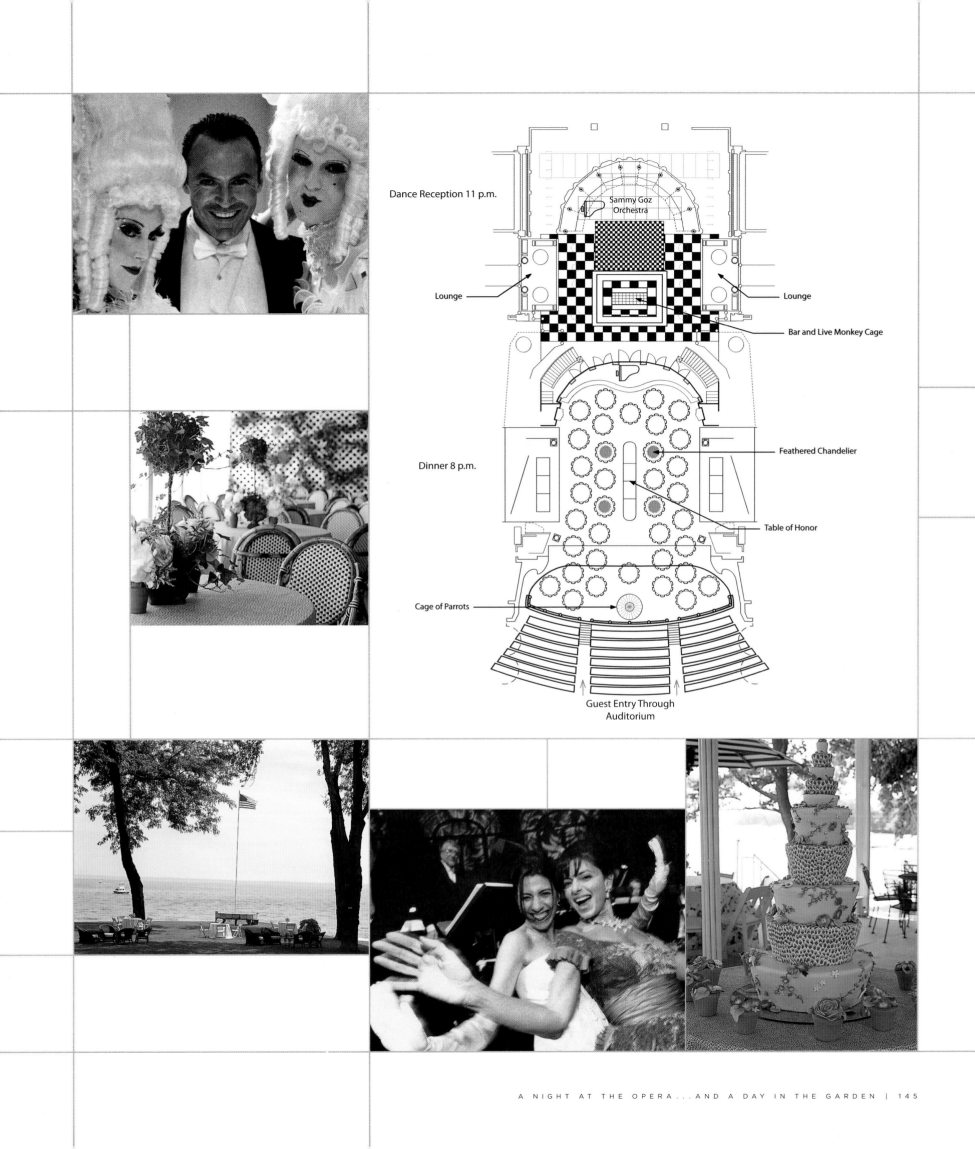

Dance Reception 11 p.m.

Sammy Goz Orchestra

Lounge

Lounge

Bar and Live Monkey Cage

Feathered Chandelier

Dinner 8 p.m.

Table of Honor

Cage of Parrots

Guest Entry Through Auditorium

READY...SET...DRAMA!

Never, ever give away all your surprises at once. Withhold. Reveal. Withhold again. Now: Dazzle your guests at a point in the evening when they least expect it. Every storyteller knows that in order to tell a great story, you have to keep your listeners happily off-kilter. It's all about having a carefully well-thought-out beginning, middle, and end. This is another way of saying that you should give your guests what they want—but always do it in an original, unexpected way. Allow the inherent drama of the evening to gradually take shape . . . build . . . then *peak*! before the event winds

its way back down to a gloriously unexpected finale.

Example: We began serving drinks in the foyer of the Met, allowing our guests to become accustomed to the costumed guards who would accompany us through the evening like a chorus. Once our guests were onstage and had absorbed their extraordinary surroundings, we deftly lowered the chandeliers and brought out the silver cloches.

Imagine: A half hour earlier, if you'd asked most guests what was going to happen next, they might have met your gaze quizzically. *Isn't this enough?* None sus-

pected that twenty-five feet away lay in wait an equally unforgettable after-party . . . until the backdrop rose to reveal our unforgettable Act Three. Monkeys? Feathers? Black patent-leather chairs? A twenty-one-piece orchestra? Who knew?

The most crucial element of any party is also the least costly: timing. Timing is what gives a great party its production value. From the moment guests alight from their cars, we want to shepherd them through an uninterrupted fantasy. Before they can glance down at their watches, get the next activity under way.

GET ON THE FLOOR!

Any good foundation stems from a first-rate floor plan. In order to follow your event schedule, you must have a floor plan that clearly demonstrates not only where each activity will be taking place, but where it's going to be set up. Every single event I create has a floor plan that is tested out by the caterer, the lighting designer, the

florist, and, of course, myself, to ensure it will be a smashing success.

Ask yourself: How many tables will I use? What shape will they be? Will they be long, round, or a mixture of the two? Where will I (and my family) sit? How will I light the room? Where will the band perform? Many banquet

facilities have existing floor plans that you can custom-modify. There are also a handful of computer programs that help you draw up plans for both the ceremony and for seating. In effect, you can become—in addition to wearing the hats of producer, director, and screenwriter—your own scenic designer.

PUTTING IT TOGETHER

Just as a wedding is (ideally) divided into three distinct acts, your wedding planning should also consist of three distinct parts: pre-production, the party, and post-production.

For pre-production, you should itemize every single major delivery and time-sensitive element—the arrival of the cake, the installation of the flowers and lighting, the arrival of hair and makeup artists, the music selections and/or bands. Everything (and everyone) should be ready to go in anticipation of the first guest's arrival.

When will the boutonnieres and bouquets be delivered? From where will the bride and her father enter? When will the organist sound out the first chords of the

processional march? What appetizers will be passed during the cocktail reception? When will the speeches take place? When will the cake be cut? If you're able to choreograph a sequence of events, and lay out the plots, subplots, and the who-does-what-when (and give copies of this schedule to all your vendors), you can actually "attend" your wedding before a single guest shows up.

My general rule of thumb is that the wedding ceremony should begin no more than fifteen minutes after the time printed on the invitation.

Another general rule of thumb: The cocktail "hour" should last no longer than forty-five minutes, keeping in mind that it will take at least fifteen minutes to transition

your guests from cocktails to the main reception. Dinner should be served as soon as possible, followed by the cutting of the cake.

A good alternative? Before dinner is served, bring guests into the reception room for a short set of dancing. Next, serve the meal. The dance portion of the party then follows. Dancing between courses makes for an extremely long service.

Post-production is just as critical as pre-production. The venue should be left exactly as it was found. This typically necessitates everything from returning tablecloths and floral vessels to rental companies, to taking down and packing up the lighting.

ONCE UPON A WEDDING

SANTA BARBARA, CALIFORNIA

October 16, 2004

When our groom first met his bride, he immediately discovered that her beauty was matched only by her incredible heart and character. Having immigrated on her own to the United States from South America, the bride had worked hard, saving enough money to support her family before even considering doing anything for herself. Royalty comes in many forms, and the groom knew this. He fell head over heels in love with her, as only an American prince can.

As good luck would have it, a longtime friend of the couple (who considers them her family) made the pair a generous offer: Would they allow her to host the wedding on her estate outside of Santa Barbara? Would they! They would be honored. Nestled in the towering mountains within view of Los Padres National Forest, the estate, with its own private redwood forest, sprawling lawns, reflecting pond, and towering fountain, was the ideal fairy-tale setting for a groom and his princess. With natural beauty like this at our disposal, I was privileged to be able to dream up a fabulous, dramatic celebration in tribute to two extraordinary people, and their 250 friends and family members who were flying in from all over the country and South America.

Friday night's rehearsal dinner took place at Mollie's Trattoria, a coastal restaurant that serves the most delicious Italian cuisine, including the best meatballs on the planet. In this romantic, candlelit setting—and serenaded by an accordionist—guests took their seats at three very long tables with terra-cotta-colored cloths that draped to the ground. We'd covered the tabletops with beautifully embroidered Renaissance-style linen overlays, on which I'd placed several different varieties of red roses in shapely terra-cotta pots, magnums of Tuscan wine, and countless amber votives mixed among a series of elegant creamy candles on antique iron stands. Home-cooked by Mollie, the dinner was served family-style, with platter after platter overflowing with pastas, chicken, foccacia bread, herb-flecked tomatoes with basil and mozzarella, and, of course, miles of Mollie's famous meatballs.

It was a warm and heartfelt welcome to a supremely beautiful wedding weekend.

Late the next afternoon, as the sun was beginning to move behind the mountains, guests arrived at a reception area tucked within the hostess's private redwood forest. A quartet of

classical violinists serenaded them, while a team of waiters served glistening nonalcoholic blood-orange juice cocktails and sparkling water. Within the forest, I'd managed to custom-create an enchanted glade, overflowing with all the shapes, colors, textures, and moods of fall. Soft Irish and Scotch mosses, dotted with miniature amber rose plants, carpeted the forest's rocks and boulders, and cornucopias of pumpkins, squashes, and fanciful gourds spilled over from brown-wicker trumpets onto tangles of wild vines. Hand-opened coral roses suspended from the redwood boughs on single strands of monofilament lent a starry, otherworldly touch to the setting. The hostess's extraordinary property consists of a house whose spectacular lawn continues on as far as the eye can see, punctuated only by an immense pond and a giant white fountain, then continuing its forward sweep. I'd created three separate seating areas on the expansive lawn, with extravagant floral gazebos connecting the two aisles, each containing all the colors of autumn. Candles and simple flowers floated serenely around the white fountain in the nearby pond; thus, from where they were sitting, guests could glance back . . . but I'm getting ahead of myself.

The officiant in charge of the wedding ceremony was author and spiritual adviser Dr. Marianne Williamson. Once she, the groom, and the rest of the bridal party were in position under the arbor of flowers, there was absolute silence. No sights or sounds other than a wind picking up, the clouds moving overhead, and the rustling trees. Then, as one, guests suddenly overheard the faintest echoing sound. *Clip-clop. Clip-clop.* Five hundred ears perked.

Five hundred eyes lifted—and widened as the distant vision before us paused in the driveway: a figure in white, seated in a white horse-drawn carriage. The carriage moved on, the *clip-clopping* resuming, this time behind the trees (I'd discreetly positioned a microphone beneath the carriage, as well as speakers in the redwoods leading to our wedding area).

At last, the white team reappeared, bearing the bride. She looked resplendent in stunning Vera Wang couture, holding a bouquet of French lace garden roses. As the carriage came into sight, four trumpeters, their instruments draped with beautiful white satin fabric initialed with the bride and groom's logo, announced her arrival with a royal fanfare, followed by "Trumpet Voluntary." The bride alighted from the carriage, then made her way down the aisle to join the wedding party under the gazebo, which was adorned in autumnal colored roses—oranges, golds, pale pinks, and aubergines—as an eight-piece string section serenaded her with Gounod's "Avé Maria."

The sheer beauty of our setting—the musicians, the flowers, the distant, fog-laced mountains, the setting sun—and, of course, the obvious love between the bride and groom made for a ceremony no one would ever forget. At the same time, no one expected what came next. As Reverend Williamson pronounced "You may kiss the bride," the enormous twenty-five-foot-high white fountain erupted like Mount Vesuvius in jetting cascades of high-flying water . . . as the four trumpeters reappeared to sound out a second fanfare . . . as four waiters strode forward and, with thrusts of their sabers (yes, sabers!), cleanly and simultaneously sliced off

the tops of jeroboams of Perrier-Jouët "flower bottles," pouring the foaming contents into a trio of magnificent pyramidal champagne fountains. Now, *that's* a fairy-tale moment to remember!

Following the ceremony, a classical trio played as guests feasted on foie gras with stone fruit chutney, seared scallops with truffle-and-corn risotto, tuna tartare with quail egg, chicken croquettes with tomato fondue, and amazing caviar served on Chinese spoons.

The bride and groom made their way to the dinner tent in the horse-drawn carriage, narrowly beating the rumored forecast of an early-evening downpour. With the help of a trolley car straight from San Francisco, we transported our 250 guests from the cocktail reception to the spectacular dinner tent.

A stone path illuminated with authentic park lamps and wrought-iron-and-wood benches led our guests to the beautiful entrance. Whenever I design, I like to make structures look as authentic as possible. In this instance, instead of a huge white tent sitting in the middle of the lawn, I'd created a more organic feel to our tent by wrapping a balcony around its sides, which I'd created especially from wooden trellises woven with intricate vines, clusters of grapes, and blooming roses, punctuated with wall sconces. Thanks to strategically placed wicker furniture and romantic lighting, the atmosphere was truly inviting—as was the tent's sumptuous interior. The ceiling was draped in olive taffeta, and the glamorous jeweled gold chandelier created a natural focal point for our sunken, circular dance floor. The tent's walls were covered with green silk, with thick wooden crown molding that circled the room. Velvet columns punctuated the walls, and authentic cottage-pane doorways led guests back outside to the balcony. Our tables were dressed with hand-beaded floral silk overlays, with underlays of olive-green silk. Hydrangeas, orchids, lilies, and multicolored roses spilled over from gilded metal vessels lined with moss. We'd had the chairs slipcovered in olive-green velvet, and piped in matte-olive satin, while the head-table chair covers were monogrammed with the bride and groom's conjoined initials.

Guest chef Geoffrey Zakarian from New York's famous Town restaurant prepared one of the most savory, memorable meals anyone could imagine. Guests started off with a kabocha squash puree with brown butter croutons, followed by a salad of chicory with Anjou pear and King Island blue cheese in a light muscat vinaigrette. The main course was just as delectable, with aged Niman Ranch rib eye with bone marrow soufflé; wild spinach puree and cherry spoon bread; and for a pre-cake-cutting enticement, apple and *Dolci di Latte* caramel toffee mousse with blackberry sorbet and vanilla ice cream. Our dinner was accompanied by a trio of fine wines.

Finally, there was the cake, which confectioner extraordinaire Sam Godfrey of Perfect Endings created—a truly amazing, towering masterpiece inspired by my fabrics and flowers, and divided with a pair of ornate miniature cages inspired by the gorgeous ironwork surrounding the tent. It was one of the most beautiful wedding cakes I have ever seen.

For the first dance? It came as a surprise treat when the legendary Roberta Flack came out to serenade slow-dancing guests with her own legendary "The First Time Ever I Saw Your Face." When guests had dried their eyes (that song can make grown men bawl under any circumstances, much less at a wedding reception), the L.A.-based band Soulville hit the stage for the after-party and had guests jiving on the dance floor all night long. By this time there was a torrential rain storm outside, but nothing was going to stop this group from having a good time.

When the evening finally came to an end, guests bided the time while waiting for their cars by sipping steaming mugs of hot chocolate, and admiring their parting gift: a miniature cake inspired by the design of the show-stopping wedding cake they'd tasted just hours earlier. Each mini-confection was the same flavor as the wedding cake, with a bottom tier of red velvet, and candy-bar flavoring for the top two. The sweetest possible ending to a fairy-tale extravaganza.

MENU

FOIE GRAS

with Stone Fruit Chutney

SEARED SCALLOPS

with Truffle and Corn Risotto

TUNA TARTARE WITH QUAIL EGG

CHICKEN CROQUETTES

with Tomato Fondue

CAVIAR ON A CHINESE SPOON

∾

COSTA DE ORO "GOLD COAST" CHARDONNAY 2002

HITCHING POST "SANTA BARBARA" PINOT NOIR 2001

PERRIER-JOUËT "FLOWER BOTTLE" IN JEROBOAM

∾

KABOCHA SQUASH PUREE

with Brown Butter Croutons

∾

MARCH COLIN CHASSAGNE-MONTRACHET CHAMPS GAINS 2002

∾

SALAD OF CHICORY

with Anjou Pear and King Island Blue Cheese in a Light Muscat Vinaigrette

∾

AGED NIMAN RANCH RIB EYE

with Bone Marrow Soufflé

WILD SPINACH PUREE AND CHERRY SPOON BREAD

∾

JORDAN CABERNET SAUVIGNON 2000

APPLE AND *DOLCI DI LATTE*

CARAMEL TOFFEE MOUSSE

with Blackberry Sorbet and Vanilla Ice Cream

∾

BILLECART-SALMON BRUT ROSÉ, NV

WEDDING CAKE

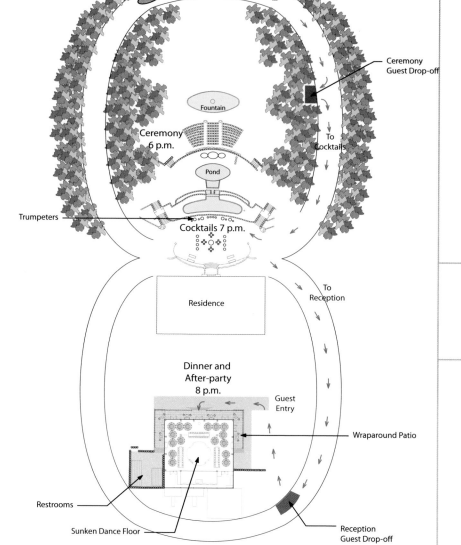

Ximena Diez-Barroso and Alejandro Adrete

LOS CABOS, MEXICO

APRIL 3, 2004

Some brides like to preside over every detail of their special day while others are happy to sit back and let me do the heavy lifting. But planning Ximena and Alejandro's wedding was very much a family affair. Ximena's father, Fernando, and stepmother, Mary Lou, envisioned a weekend that would be their once-in-a-lifetime gift to the happy couple—a dream wedding filled with family, friends, food, music, and, of course, a liberal dollop of magic.

Although the bride's parents live in Los Angeles and abroad, the celebration would take place in her father's native Mexico, where he is a prominent businessman, and where much of his (and the groom's) extended family lives. Mary Lou, who is Italian, would have relatives flying in from Italy, and naturally, many guests would be arriving from the West Coast. We quickly zeroed in on Los Cabos, at the southernmost tip of the Baja Peninsula. Its central location and easy airport access would be convenient for our international travelers, and its brand-new Los Cabos Marquis Hotel could accommodate all 450 guests. Even better, we'd have exclusive use of the hotel for the entire weekend!

At six P.M. on Friday evening, 150 of the couple's nearest and dearest friends gathered in the Marquis's Presidential Suite for a quiet civil ceremony to legalize Ximena and Alejandro's marriage, as is the custom in Mexico. The pair sat at a long table blanketed in rose petals, and glowing with candlelight, while the judge officiated over the signing of the marriage documents. Following this brief ceremony, everyone headed downstairs to meet up with the rest of the guests, who'd been checking into the hotel throughout the day, greeted with a beautifully wrapped candle, a gardenia blossom, and a welcome-note.

To showcase our stunning surroundings—the whitewashed walls of the hotel, the aquamarine of the water, the electric hues of a Baja sunset and night sky—we honed in on one singularly sensational idea: coral. I've always loved coral, and so, it turns out, did Ximena and Mary Lou. We agreed to make it the central theme for our party, incorporating both the plant's vibrant color and fabulous sculptural quality into seating, tables, and centerpieces. We were determined to "coralize Los Cabos!"—and the results were sexy, sleek, and modern.

At seven P.M., led by the finest mariachis we could find, Ximena and Alejandro descended the steps from the lobby to the poolside patio, where their guests and an exquisite feast

awaited them. In deference to Mary Lou's heritage, and as a surprise change from the Mexican cuisine everyone was expecting, we had decided to create an enchanting Italian dinner on six buffet tables, each with a tall manzanita branch painted in coral and decorated with a beaded lamp shade. The key tonight was *abundance*. We also set up two gorgeous seafood buffets at the edge of the pool, where guests were treated to platefuls of fresh, locally caught prawns, lobsters, mussels, jumbo shrimp, stone crab claws, Alaskan king crab legs, and oysters, served by barefoot servers standing directly in the pool, in ankle-deep water, with the legs of their tuxedo pants rolled up. It was a great beachy touch. Guests could also help themselves to the salmon station, which was overflowing with ceviche, quenelles, and delicately smoked salmon fillets, sliced angel-wing-thin, as well as sample some over-the-top charcuterie—an elaborate array of salami, mortadella, prosciutto, soppressata, bresaola, you name it. But few people missed out on our main entrée, a juicy roasted breast of veal with a crunchy crust of herbs, as well as our extraordinary selection of artisanal cheeses and enough decadent desserts to satisfy any sweet tooth, such as individual cups of chocolate *pot de crème,* biscotti and chocolate fondue, and strawberry soup with champagne and sorbet. A selection of extraordinary red wines complemented the herb-crusted veal, ports paired up with the cheeses, and delicate dessert wines finished this magnificent meal.

My team had housed the buffets for most of the courses in seven small canvas pavilions, trimmed in our phenomenally vivacious shade of coral. Inside each pavilion, a cooler and a warmer kept extra food fresh and handy for the servers to replenish trays. This little detail prevented the waitstaff from having to shuttle food back and forth in plain sight (a practice I've never liked). It also protected the food from the elements and established a uniform color scheme for all the food to come.

To take advantage of the patio's serpentine shape, I created a pair of bars in the round, and dressed them in the same coral-trimmed theme, this time using colored Plexiglas instead of canvas. We formed several seating styles and arrangements at varying heights, including a line of chaise longues placed end to end and slipcovered in coral so that they resembled one long banquette snaking its way along the interior perimeter of the patio. Low Lucite tables, lit from within by battery-operated flashlights, and coral-colored pod seats were spaced evenly opposite the banquette, creating a sophisticated spot where people could mix, dine, and chat. We'd have plenty of flowers over the next two days, so for this party, I topped each table with a tall glass cylinder filled with water and a charming, colorful goldfish.

Finally, projected on one of the adjacent hotel walls and the pool deck was an eye-popping moving design of abstract coral patterns. Lighting is, of course, atmosphere's best friend. The coral, rose, and tangerine glow juxtaposed against the deep teal of the water was seductive, audacious, and—why not?—extremely cool.

The next day, while guests toured Los Cabos, we finished putting the final touches on the site where the religious ceremony would be held. It was to be an unusually special event, as Ximena's family had arranged to have the archbishop of Mexico preside as the officiant. Having an archbishop in one's midst turned out to be quite an elaborate affair. Apparently, when the archbishop attends, he comes with a full entourage. This, coupled with the fact that it's virtually unheard of for a Catholic priest to perform a wedding outside of an actual church, made it essential that the site be as lovely and spiritual as possible.

The pressure was on—but I had a remarkable space to work with. The Marquis's main lobby is designed in an arc, with an open back end overlooking a reflecting pool and the ocean beyond. At the center of the lobby was a square cement planter that—I knew—wasn't going anywhere. Planter notwithstanding, we removed all signs of the hotel, and transformed it into our wedding ceremony arena. This meant clearing out every piece of furniture and arranging for the chairs, which were slipcovered in mint green and sage organza, to face the ocean. The aisle ran down the middle and around the planter, which we turned into a centerpiece of floating gardenias and white candles, interspersed with large tropical monstera leaves. On the hotel lobby desks, we placed pomanders of white roses and fresh limes. Tall spindles of greenery filled with fragrant freesias, gardenias, and crisp white roses stood at attention at the front of the seating area, and would serve as a backdrop for the mariachi musicians. Along the aisle we stretched a runner custom-painted with a Florentine-inspired border. Hurricane lanterns illuminated the pathway, and on the backs of all the chairs were small crystal and copper-wire cones brimming with rose petals to toss at the bride and groom after the ceremony. To add a touch of drama, we built a walkway that led several feet out into the reflecting pool and connected with the large stage that would accommodate the "floating altar." The ceremony would appear to be adrift on a sea of love.

But that wasn't all. Over the stage, we built a breathtaking arch of white roses that mimicked and reflected the shape of the arch of the hotel lobby. Suspended from our arch was an absolutely striking cross made of crystals threaded with fishing nylon. This lovely, iridescent cross positively sparkled in the evening light reflecting off the ocean. And when the sun finally set, it glimmered in the moonlight. Its haunting, shimmering transparency precisely

captured the elegance and solemnity of the religious ceremony without detracting from the grandeur and over-the-top beauty of the Baja landscape. We had even personalized the vestments by embroidering them in the same Florentine pattern as the runner, then monogrammed them with the couple's initials, the words *Los Cabos,* and the date. No detail was left unaddressed.

Ximena seemed delighted, and looked stunning in her Candace Solomon strapless A-line dress as she made her way down the aisle on the arm of her very proud father. It's always gratifying to witness two people unite their destinies, but (I must admit) nothing gave me more pleasure that day than the archbishop's sermon. He looked around for a moment, then remarked that the site we'd chosen reflected God's land. Mission accomplished!

The cocktail reception followed immediately after the service, just beyond the trellis wall outside the wedding arena. We set up nine tables with umbrellas, each of which was hand-stenciled with the now-signature Florentine design. We even projected the design on the adjacent wall of the hotel. Instead of traditional centerpieces, we draped sheaths of green

cymbidium, snow-white roses, and creamy white orchids from the poles beneath the umbrellas. Time flew deliriously past, and now Ximena and Alejandro's guests began making their way to the ballroom for dinner.

One of the challenges in designing the dinner venue was overcoming the sterile "ballroom" feeling of the room. Fortunately, I'd received permission to give the ballroom and adjoining space a complete makeover. To beckon guests into the room, and break up (as well as warm up) the space at the same time, I positioned an immense gilded screen a few feet in from the double-door entry, obliging people to enter the room from either the left or the right. The orchestra, which typically would have been set up against the far wall of such a room, was situated on the other side of this screen, facing the long table of honor opposite a large square dance floor. We reversed the expectation.

In such a long, rectangular space, guests can run the risk of feeling as though they've been cut off from the action in the center of the room. Rather than giving anyone the sense that they'd been banished to Siberia, I employed a trick I often use to create an intimate setting.

I constructed two sets of risers enclosed by custom-made gilded railings that would house the tables at different levels. The first level placed the round tables a foot above the dance floor, and the second level placed the long tables an additional foot higher. I also used caramel satin draping toward the center of the room, which I anchored with a spectacular crystal chandelier to draw everyone's attention inward. Tall mirrors situated at either end of the room reflected everything across the space. Even the choice of mixed table shapes helped contribute to the dynamic feel of a setting. First, it kept things from looking mass-produced, and second, I find that older guests prefer the intimacy of sitting at smaller round tables, while younger guests love the festive feel of the long tables.

In either case, all our tables were topped with one of two styles of overlays. On the long tables, we had a gold damask underlay and an opulent mint, emerald-green, and gold beaded overlay with heavy brocade trim. The round tables had gold damask cloths that hung to the ground, topped by olive-green silk overlays finished with charming scalloped edges. The gold ballroom chairs had matching tufted olive-green cushions. The place settings consisted of gold chargers flanked by gilded flatware and crystal glasses. On top of the chargers were lightly starched embroidered hemstitch linen napkins and menu cards bordered in the evening's trademark Florentine design, and bound with green ribbon and fresh gardenias. We incorporated a variety of centerpieces, using combinations of gold candelabras, crystal candelabras, small gold floral containers, votives, and, of course, luscious orchids, roses, magnolias, and tulips. The look was very old-world European, a stark contrast to the previous evening's contemporary Mexican theme.

The bride had made one thing clear to me during our first meeting: Elaborate decor was fine, but she did not want "complicated" food at her wedding. She wanted excellence without fuss. Given the fact that she owns a marvelous Los Angeles restaurant of her own and attended an acclaimed cooking school, I took her request very seriously, and asked chef Geoffrey Zakarian of New York City's famed Town and Country restaurants to design a menu that would suit her style. Geoffrey has never let me down, and that night would be no exception, as the food was superb.

The meal was light and summery, completely appropriate and perfectly elegant. It began with a course of silky, chilled cauliflower bisque garnished with Beluga caviar and cucumber cream. The second course was a lightly roasted striped bass dusted with candied fennel and

pink grapefruit essence. Our third course was a pinenut-and-rosemary clafoutis with an olive oil gelato and crispy praline, all accompanied by Dom Pérignon 1990 champagne. Cutting the cake, which was beautifully designed in our elegant Florentine pattern, and garnished with edible gold leaves, by genius baker Polly Schoonmaker, seemed almost criminal, but we had miles to go before we slept, and it would all begin post-cake.

Just before midnight, we invited our guests to move on to an extravagantly fun after-party. And at 12:01, it was all *cha-cha-cha*! Some seniors stayed behind in the dining room, where the orchestra continued to play. But when we planned the wedding, Ximena told me that she and Alejandro wanted to dance the night away in a fabulous, chic nightclub. Since the hotel didn't have one, it was up to us to put one together. What we came up with had to have been, that night, the hottest spot in all of Mexico.

The hotel generously gave us the use of its adjacent business center, so we had the ideal space. But it was sorely in need of help to get it to the funky stratosphere. I'd painted the ceiling gold, and the walls a lively apple green. We brought in a large gold leather bar from which Dale DeGroff, one of the most celebrated cocktail movers and shakers in the world, could serve his most legendary concoctions. A great big dance floor at the center of the room seemed to whirl in the kaleidoscopic lights of fifteen fantastic, different-sized disco balls hanging from above. We had sleek banquettes and couches covered in turquoise silk with corresponding tiger-print skin. A tiered dessert station (imagine every cookie, macaroon,

and candied jelly known to mankind) was covered in those same fabrics. Glowing Lucite tables, such as the ones we'd used for our poolside coral party, provided spots for Ximena and Alejandro's friends to linger over drinks.

Speaking of drinks, this party arrived with its own signature cocktail. I'd asked Dale to come up with something that, after a long dinner, would get everyone in the mood to dance and give them a shot of energy. What he delivered was the drink to end all drinks: two parts tequila, one part espresso, and a liberal sprinkling of Tia Maria, all tossed into a martini shaker, then poured into shot glasses rimmed in orange oil, powdered chocolate, and chili pepper. Believe me, if you're looking to jump-start a party, that's definitely the winning solution! Still, sometimes the heart says, "Dance!" while the feet whimper, "No can do." For those unfortunate soles, we passed out cushiony slippers and brought in a masseuse trained in the heavenly art of foot massage. Want more? You got it! Trays of three A.M. breakfast sandwiches and five A.M. orange juice, coffee, Bloody Marys, and bullshots kept people partying until seven in the morning, when even the bride and groom had to admit it was time to call it a dazzling, dizzying, gloriously rollicking night.

Those who stayed for the whole after-party had only about three hours of rest before the celebration continued with the next morning's farewell brunch at ten-thirty. There, guests enjoyed freshly squeezed tomato juice, *huevos rancheros, huevos Mexicanos,* and a few more coral-colored memories that will last for the rest of their lives.

PROJECTING AN IMAGE

Sometimes a single visual element is all you need to spark the idea for a party's theme. Such was the case for Ximena and Alejandro's "Coralizing Los Cabos" pre-wedding welcome soiree. The resulting contrast of the deep red-orange hue against the aquamarine pools, stark white hotel exterior, and setting sun was absolutely sublime. It remains one of the most inspired, yet organic, looks I've ever created for an event.

But be careful not to go overboard when making an element the defining focus of your party's look. Too much coral and "Coralizing Los Cabos" could have turned into a "Coralized Catastrophe." Keep these tips in mind when weaving a visual theme into the look of your event:

Ceremonies and celebrations should all stem from the heart. I much prefer to work with couples who have colorful lives that they are willing to inject into their celebrations.

The more personal the celebration, the better time your guests will have. The era of the textbook wedding has come and gone. The strongest theme today is personalization.

If you collect majolica porcelains, use your collection for the centerpieces. If you have a favorite color, use it abundantly. If you both come from different cultural backgrounds, weave traditional rituals into your ceremony, which will give your family and friends a window into your cultural heritage. For more ideas about incorporating rituals into your festivities, follow Dr. Linda Garbett's advice on page 63.

MENU

FRIDAY NIGHT WELCOME RECEPTION

LOBSTER TAILS, OYSTERS, CLAMS, ALASKAN
KING CRAB LEGS,

Poached Jumbo Shrimp, and Stone Crab Claws

∾

SCOTTISH SMOKED SALMON, NORWEGIAN
CURED GRAVLAX,

Salmon Ceviche, and Salmon Tartare

∾

SOPPRESSATA, SALAMI, BRESAOLA,

and Prosciutto di Parma

FROZEN TEST TUBES OF VODKA AND AQUAVIT

SAUVIGNON BLANC

∾

ROASTED BREAST OF VEAL

with Provençal Vegetables

∾

ARTISANAL CHEESE SELECTION

CHOCOLATE *POTS DE CRÈME*

TROPICAL FRUIT SALAD

with Lime Sorbet

BISCOTTI AND
CHOCOLATE FONDUE

STRAWBERRY SOUP WITH
CHAMPAGNE AND SORBET

HOMEMADE FRESH
MARSHMALLOWS

DESSERT WINES, SPARKLING WINES,
GOURMET COFFEE

SATURDAY NIGHT WEDDING RECEPTION

TUNA TARTARE/MUSTARD OIL/

Green Apple/Crisp Rice Tuile

∾

GOAT CHEESE PROFITEROLES

with Black Olives and Pesto

∾

CRAB CAKES

∾

BLACK TRUFFLE/ONION AND BACON

en Croute

∾

MINIATURE CROQUES MONSIER

∾

CHILLED CAULIFLOWER BISQUE

with Beluga Caviar and Cucumber Cream

∾

ROASTED STRIPED BASS

with Candied Fennel and Fresh Grapefruit Essence

∾

PINENUT ROSEMARY CLAFOUTIS

with Olive Oil Gelato and Crispy Praline

∾

WEDDING CAKE

DOM PÉRIGNON 1990 CHAMPAGNE

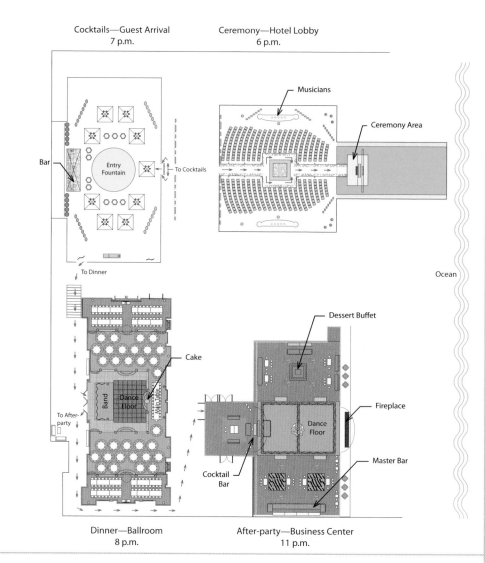

Cocktails—Guest Arrival
7 p.m.

Ceremony—Hotel Lobby
6 p.m.

Dinner—Ballroom
8 p.m.

After-party—Business Center
11 p.m.

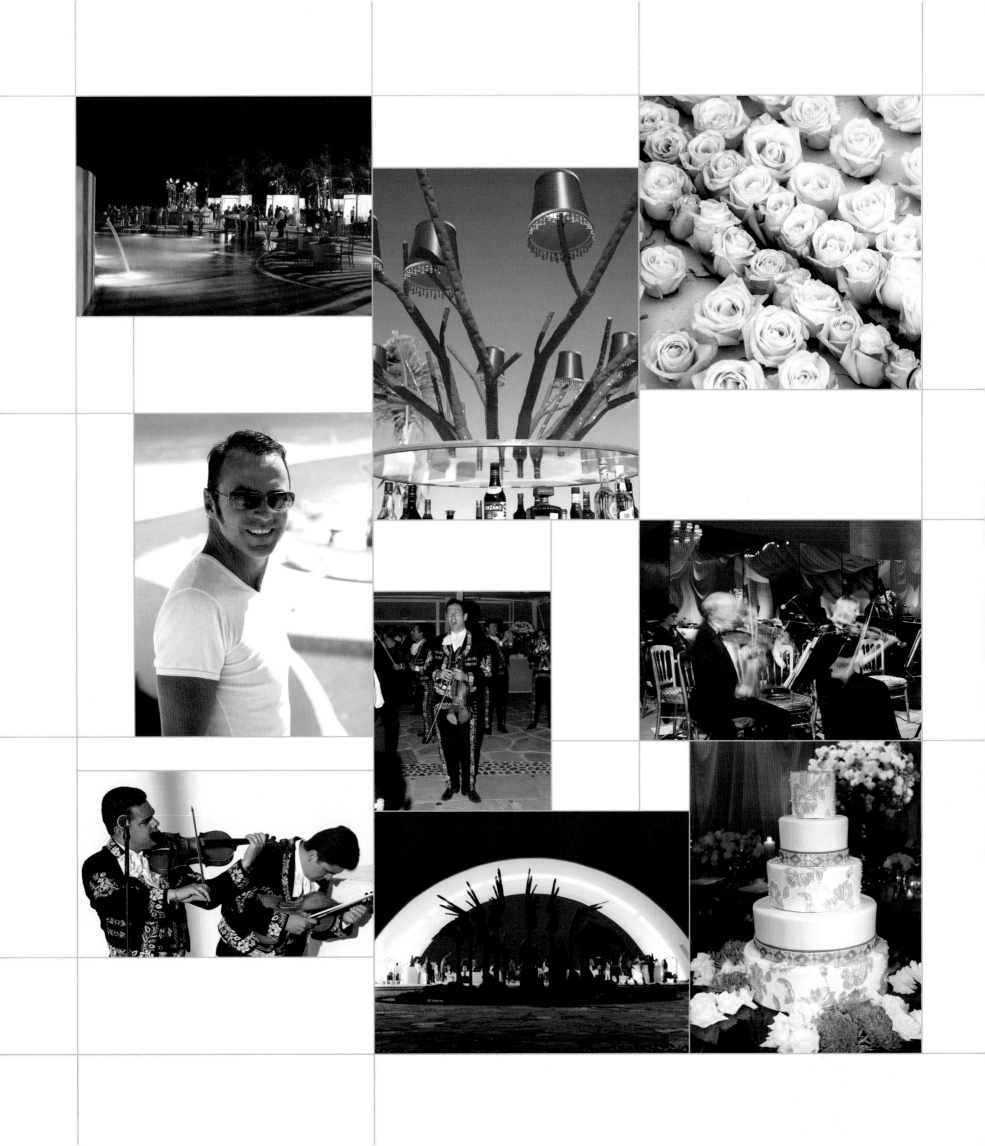

CIAO, BELLA!

VENICE, ITALY

July 10, 1999

"*There* is nothing more to be said about Venice," Henry James once observed. All I can say in reply is: He hadn't had the great fortune to arrange a wedding there.

The very private bride and groom, longtime lovers of *la dolce vita,* wanted nothing more than to get married in this most romantic and exotic of Italian cities. In the course of a preliminary scouting trip, they showed me every out-of-the-way sight and scene they loved the most. I began to understand that Venice, with its tides, lagoons, canals, *calli, campi, palazzi,* and *ponti,* not to mention its amazing artistic, architectural, literary, and cinematic history, was an integral part of their identities, their romance, their history together. With apologies to Henry James, there was a *lot* more to say about Venice.

Moreover, the bride and groom wanted their friends and family members to revel in the city they knew and adored. Not the Venice of tourist brochures—of gondolas, pigeons, and tourist-clogged piazzas—but a behind-the-scenes Venice that had slowly revealed itself to them over the years.

I was thrilled to be able to plot and carry out my first Italian wedding. Venice has had its share of glittering, magical heydays, but for me, one of its most evocative eras took place in the 1950s, an era I associate with glamorous Hollywood movies—swan-necked actresses in saucer-sized dark glasses, sipping champagne in gondolas, or speeding across the lagoon to the Lido Beach Hotel, their scarves flapping in the wind, a fatally charming Romeo at the wheel.

We thought it would be fun to play around with the traditional order of events. Friday night's black-tie rehearsal dinner at the Palazzo Pisani Moretta would be our opulent, over-the-top blowout. Saturday would be a free day (though the bride and groom had some great, insider-ly recommendations). The wedding itself would be a simple sunset ceremony on Saturday evening in the gardens of the Hotel Cipriani, across the lagoon from St. Mark's Square, capped off with a chic 1950s-era dinner dance inside the hotel. If that weren't enough, the bride and groom would host a farewell poolside brunch on Sunday.

July is notorious as being the most popular, crowded month in Venice. Even with a full nine months to plan our Italian wedding weekend, we had to negotiate and renegotiate to get space in the hotels we wanted for our guests. Ultimately, we were able to reserve guest rooms at the Hotel Cipriani, the Hotel Danieli, the Gritti Palace, and the Hotel Europa.

Designer Marc Friedland immediately went to work on our save-the-date cards, producing a thick card stock in a palette of robin's-egg blue (it perfectly matched the bride's ice-blue John Galliano–designed wedding gown), with sable-brown ink and a brown-backed silver border adorned with a matte silver lining. Each oversized invitation was crowned with an Art Deco–style monogram of the bride's and groom's initials, an insignia that became his/her own signature throughout the three-day celebration.

Once we received the RSVPs, we sent off our confirmation packages. These contained everything from a list of airlines, to the travel agent's contact information, to an itinerary of weekend events, to a dress code, even directions for transport to the various hotels. A final stylish touch: coded luggage tags that allowed for a seamless and utterly stress-free transfer.

While guests were busy making their travel plans, our production team was working feverishly to ensure that our guests would enjoy smooth sailing from the day of their arrival to their departure. We knew that guests at destination weddings sometimes worry when they have never been to the locale in question and, in many cases, don't speak the language. (Translation: They are *extremely* apprehensive about getting lost.) Our solution: We came up with shirts, hats, clipboards, and pins embroidered with our unmistakable wedding logo of the bride's and groom's initials.

Decked out in monogrammed wedding caps and shirts, our staff in Venice welcomed seventy jet-lagged but exhilarated guests at Venice's Marco Polo and Trevise airports, calmly shepherding them via water taxi to their hotels. As guests disembarked, they had only to spy our logo and their names on a Lucite clipboard in the hands of a waiting greeter. There couldn't have been an easier, more comforting, or less anxiety-provoking way to enter Venice.

I'd met with the room-service managers at each of our participating hotels, and they agreed to bring a welcome tray to each guest's room no later than fifteen minutes after check-in time. (If the items had been nonperishable, I would have requested they be left in the rooms before the guests arrived.) Each tray held a detailed itinerary of our upcoming weekend, adorned with a fragrant Venetian rose, ice-cold Bellinis—the world-renowned signature drink of Harry's Bar in Venice, consisting of sparkling white wine mixed with pureed white peaches—and a gorgeous bowl of ripe-to-bursting red cherries ("Life is just a bowl of cherries!" the bride once exclaimed—so why not make her words reality?). Lastly, there was a powder-blue box neatly tied with a sable grosgrain ribbon. Inside was a powder-blue and

silver-leaf Murano crystal vase tumbling over with delectable blue, silver, and white *dragées* flown in from Paris.

On Friday night, after a few hours for rest and freshening up, water taxis picked up our guests, who'd by now changed into black formal evening wear, and ferried them to the Palazzo Pisani Moretta, a fifteenth-century palace on the Grand Canal, famous for its Gothic mullioned windows and stunning baroque interior. The Palazzo was dramatically lit that night, bathed in a gentle, otherworldly light—a sneak peek at that night's palette of lavender, amethyst, and eggplant. Downstairs, two white-gloved, white-suited gentlemen assisted guests from their boats and ushered them inside, where the Venetian classical quartet known as Quaddri was already serenading the room with Italian love songs. Waiters greeted new arrivals with magnums of La Grande Dame Champagne (in honor of the occasion, Veuve Clicquot agreed to bottle La Grande Dame in a magnum size), and platters of foie gras, fresh smoked salmon, and truffles. And why limit our color palette for use in flowers and table overlays? In honor of the bride's favorite color, I'd arranged for every bottle of champagne to contain a single tiny drop of lavender food coloring.

The soon-to-be-newlyweds arrived in a stylish speedboat that had seats I'd gotten specially reupholstered in linen, and their initials embossed on the hull. A beautiful garland of red roses trailed in the lagoon behind them like a floral wedding train. Even the captain's cap and the flag on the boat were custom-stitched and embossed with the wedding logo.

Taking my cue from the gorgeous lace and blue hues of the bride's wedding gown, I'd dressed the tables in intricate and lavish laces, lamés, and damasks of the same color. Our centerpieces, spilling over with grapes, roses, and amaranths, oozed baroque luxuriousness. It was as if they were stretching upward to join the twelve ceiling candelabras, whose white candles shimmered and flickered across the ceiling and tabletops. A perfect comple-ment to this elegant, centuries-old atmosphere was the costumed members of Rondo Veneziano, a music ensemble that combines the splashy stylings of Vivaldi with an utterly enticing modern beat.

Our Cipriani-catered dinner was classic formal Venetian redesigned for American palates. For example: Instead of arranging a carpaccio of sea bass flat on a plate, we trans-formed our fish into a three-dimensional basil-infused tower atop a crisp bed of fennel and green apples. This was followed by a creamy risotto with scampi and zucchini blossoms, a chilled cherry tomato soup with medallions of lobster, and, finally, veal rosettes with Marsala wine and black truffles—all accompanied by rich French and Italian wines. Throughout the evening, a photographer took each guest aside to snap a keepsake photo. After dinner, guests adjourned to an adjacent room, where an array of fine Italian cheeses, ripe fruits, crusty breads, and tawny ports awaited. The evening climaxed with Cipriani's heavenly warm chocolate cake with chocolate sorbet and chocolate sauce. An accordion player serenaded guests as they reluctantly climbed back into their boats and motored back to their hotels.

Saturday, as I mentioned, was a do-as-you-please day. Guides were available to take guests on a tour of Venice by foot or by boat, shepherd them to glass factories or museums, or pilot them across the lagoon to play a round of golf at the Lido. For those who wanted to be entirely on their own, they were secure in the knowledge that someone—in this case, a pri-vate concierge—was just a call away. Problems? Worries? Concerns? Language difficulties? We gave each guest the concierge's phone number, and the concierge was mandated to pick up the phone in two rings or less.

Before long, the day was darkening, and lights were reflecting in the choppy gray waters of the Grand Canal. It was time for our wedding.

The weather that night was moody, with off-and-on showers, raising the possibility that we might have to bring our ceremony indoors. But at last the night cleared, and we proceeded outdoors to the gardens behind the Cipriani. As instructed, every single one of our guests was attired in white linen. My team had created a large, sumptuous arbor by planting rosebushes into the earth, adorned with white flowering roses and clusters of grapes that closely mirrored a century-old arbor. By planting them directly in the ground, ours looked as though they had been growing there forever. Instead of strict formal seating, we'd created whimsical groupings of white slipcovered chairs, separated by buckets of milky rose petals placed there in anticipation of the bride's entrance. As guests took their seats, a quartet appeared for a reprise of classic Italian love songs (not to mention a rendition of "Life Is Just a Bowl of Cherries").

As the bride came out, a vision in ice blue, the scene behind the Cipriani looked like heaven. The darkening sky. The soft chop of the lagoon. Fragrant rose petals underfoot. The subtle contrast of hues couldn't have been more striking, or dramatic. Meeting up with her groom (handsomely clad in white tie), the bride proceeded to the foot of the arbor, a scattering of the lushest, snowiest rose petals surrounding them.

When the ceremony was over, guests assembled on the patio for a champagne reception, while the newlyweds, accompanied by a photographer, sped off in a boat to take photos in St. Mark's Square, at a church on the Grand Canal, and in a few other spots they found en route. Upon their return, guests retired to the Cipriani's upstairs private dining room for a dinner reception, though not before they were first regaled with a brief, brilliant fireworks show that culminated—naturally—with the bride and groom's sky-lit logo.

Upstairs at the Cipriani Hotel, our reception room exuded a glamorous, cinematic 1950s feel. The pleated white walls and ceilings and custom-dyed powder-blue carpet ideally complemented our gentle wedding palette. The tables were dressed to the ground with ice-blue bengaline and topped with starched white hemstitch overlays and matching monogrammed napkins. Our flowers—white and blue hydrangeas, and lilies of the valley—were tucked elegantly into shimmering silver Revere bowls.

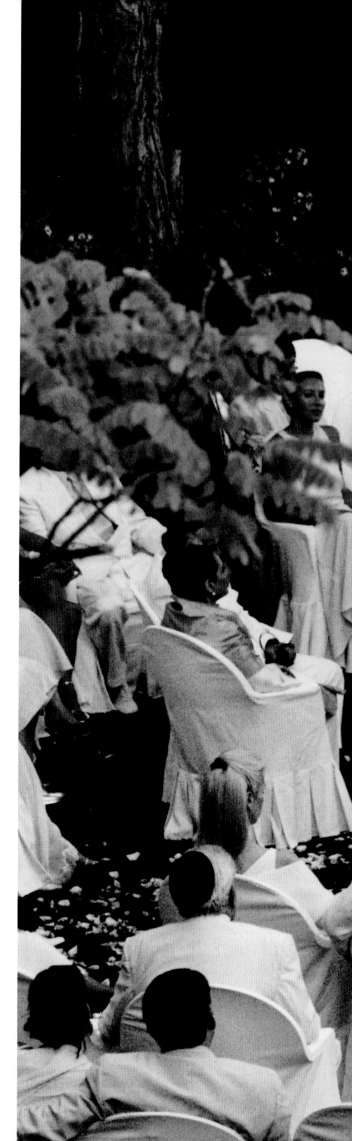

The Cipriani-catered menu was sumptuous, and included the bride and groom's favorite dishes: shrimp on a bed of frisée; a fillet of turbot with spring vegetables; Cipriani's signature baked *tagliarini verde* with ham and cream; and a luscious roasted loin of lamb with herb-and-tarragon sauce. There was a treat for guests' ears, as well. In homage to the Rat Pack hipness of the fifties, we'd flown in the Todd Londagin Orchestra, who, attired in cream suits and with their hair slicked back, serenaded the guests with pop-jazz tunes through a vintage microphone. Dancing was momentarily interrupted only by the cutting of our beautiful powder-blue and violet wedding cake. Waiters doled out slices, accompanied by cold, frothy Sgroppinos (one part vodka, one part Prosecco, one part lemon sorbet, all parts fabulous). After the bride and groom delivered two moving speeches to each other, guests resumed dancing, staying for hours into the Venetian night. As a delirious coda, waiters passed out Cuban cigars.

But the dream wasn't over for the bride and groom. As a surprise, I'd arranged for the finest 482-thread-count Pratesi sheets to envelop their bed in the Cipriani's Honeymoon Suite, embossed with their by-now-familiar wedding logo. The room itself was ankle-deep in white rose petals, with hundreds of votive candles everywhere casting a romantic glow.

Sunday's farewell brunch, held poolside, had to work overtime to match the previous forty-eight hours' worth of opulence, but it succeeded magnificently. The bar area was magnetically alive with gorgeous yellow roses and festive yellow tablecloths. As the guests helped themselves to a buffet of antipasti, frittata, pastries, and ripe fruits, there was no doubt in anyone's mind that this had been the most spectacular—most *dolce*—weekend ever for the bride, the groom, and their guests. Even Henry James would have loved it.

MENU

FRIDAY NIGHT DINNER

SELECTION OF COLD CANAPÉS
(Foie Gras, Salmon, Truffles, Carpaccio, and Vegetables)

∾

VEUVE CLICQUOT LA GRANDE DAME CHAMPAGNE

∾

MARINATED SEA BASS
with Basil on a Bed of Fennel and Green Apple Salad

∾

RISOTTO WITH SCAMPI AND ZUCCHINI BLOSSOMS

∾

COLD CHERRY TOMATO SOUP WITH LOBSTER

∾

JERMANN FRIULI VG SAUVIGNON BLANC 1997

∾

VEAL ROSETTES
with a Marsala Wine and Black Truffles from Norcia Sauce

∾

ALLEGRINI LA POJA VENETO 1998

∾

CHEESE AND FRUIT BUFFET

∾

GRAHAM THIRTY-YEAR-OLD TAWNY PORT

WARM CHOCOLATE CAKE
with Chocolate Sorbet and Chocolate Sauce

MACULAN VIGNAIULOI TORCOLATO

COFFEE WITH FRIANDISES

SATURDAY WEDDING RECEPTION

CHAMPAGNE KRUG ROSÉ

∾

SHRIMP ON BED OF SHREDDED FRISÉE
and Radicchio with Balsamic Reduction

GRATIN OF TAGHAIRINI

∾

FILET OF TURBOT
with Spring Vegetables

∾

ZUCCHINI PUREED, AU GRATIN
in White Wine Sauce

∾

RONC DI JURI, GIROLAMO DORIGO 1996

∾

ROASTED LOIN OF LAMB
with Herbs and Tarragon Sauce

BRUNELLO DI MONTALCINO "GREPPO," F. BUINDI SANTI 1994
OR BAROLO BRUNATE, BRICCO ROCCHE 1995

∾

ICED MOUSSE FLAVORED
with Grappa Picolit Nonino, Bitter Orange Sauce

∾

WEDDING CAKE

MERINGUE CAKE
with Lemon Sorbet, Fresh Berries

GRAPPA UNIVITIGNO

COFFEE AND FRIANDISES

SGROPPINO

Ceremony 7 p.m.

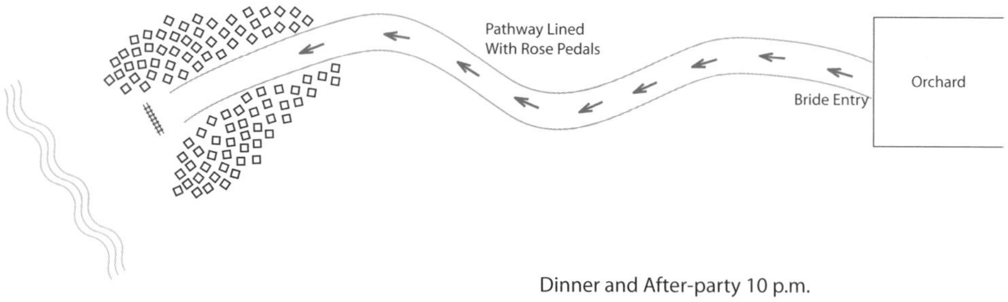

Pathway Lined With Rose Pedals

Orchard

Bride Entry

Dinner and After-party 10 p.m.

Dinner and After-party 10 p.m.

Upstairs to Reception

White Drape

Wedding Cake

White Dance Floor

Band

Windows

View of Venice

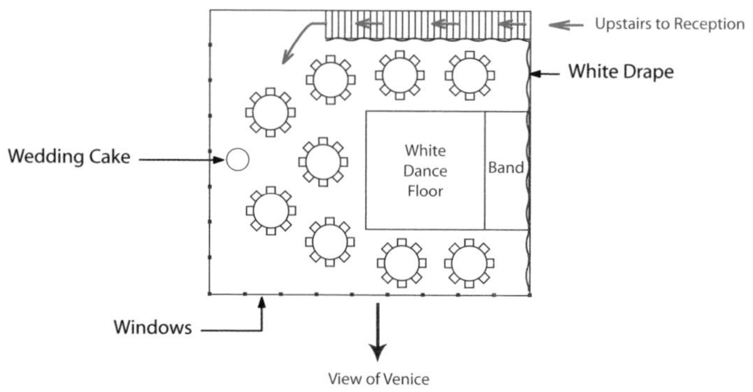

DESTINATION: HAPPINESS

A sandy Bahamian beach at sunset. An eighteenth-century palazzo. A cozy country inn deep in the New England countryside. A Hebridean castle. A leaf-strewn botanical garden tucked away in the middle of a great city. A destination wedding takes a lot of time, work, planning, and energy to bring together—but it's also an incredible opportunity to share your wedding day with a close gathering of friends and family in a dynamic setting far and beyond the traditional banquet hall, hotel ballroom, or childhood backyard. Be assured of one thing: You and your guests will never forget it.

Of course, the question is, Where? Quite often, a couple will have a specific destination in mind. It might be the seaside restaurant in Capri where they first realized they had everything in common, or the snow-capped resort where they go skiing at the end of every year. More than once, my clients have asked me to propose a location that I think captures the essence of their personalities, someplace that's not only fun and fabulous, but that doesn't take three days and four time changes' worth of travel.

Once we've zeroed in on a general area, we plan a scouting trip. Our goal is to uncover the perfect spot for the kind of wedding the couple is fantasizing about, to

get an intimate feel for the surroundings, and to discover a few things we could showcase for our guests. We might pay a visit to local merchants. We might take a tour with a native guide. Armed with a list of questions, we might check out a few hotels or resorts. Can they accommodate the number of people in our party? Does our time frame line up with theirs? Often we'll make more than one trip to get a feel for what the local vendors have to offer. Once these details are set, it's time to begin designing our celebration.

The first thing we do—without exception!—is send out save-the-date cards. Ideally, these should indicate the destination, so that guests have sufficient time to choreograph their lives and busy schedules around our event. Rather than waiting the traditional six weeks to follow up with invitations, we mail them as soon as possible. Once we receive the RSVPs, we send out confirmation packages, which include all the pertinent details: transportation, itinerary, what people should wear, when, and for what occasion.

Within the confirmation package, we give the name and contact information of a single travel agent, who can deal with any or all flight and scheduling requirements—and who'll provide guests with customized, personalized

luggage tags with our wedding logo on them. That way, they can arrive at the location secure in the knowledge that their luggage will be waiting for them upstairs in their rooms. No stress! If I've said it once, I've said it a million times: A well-informed guest is a happy guest.

Upon their arrival, we also make sure that guests have a welcome-note and gift waiting for them in their rooms. The note might acknowledge the effort friends and family have made to travel as far as they have, before going on to describe the upcoming wedding weekend, as well as a list of fun things to do in their free time. The welcome-gift might include a bottle of wine, a scented candle, and a few practical items guests can use during their stay (suntan lotion, sandals, coins for the casino).

It's also a lovely idea to surprise your guests when they least expect it. What could be chicer than to return to your hotel room after a gorgeous wedding reception to find, on your pillow, a photograph of the bride and groom in a beautiful seashell frame? Or a poem by Rumi accompanying a delicious hand-dipped chocolate? Your touches should be useful and imaginative, and also have a local flavor. Long after the wedding weekend has passed, guests will remember the effort you've made to take care of them.

EAST MEETS WEST

Adeline Fong and Michael Wilson

LANAI, HAWAII

MAY 10, 2003

When

Michael Wilson, a Bay Area techie, and Malaysian-born Adeline Fong decided to marry, they knew that they wanted to hold their wedding on the small, very private Hawaiian island of Lanai (they had a home on Maui). But once they'd picked the location, the planning came to a standstill. Adeline was having trouble finding someone to help her plan the kind of wedding she dreamed of—one marked by traditional Chinese-Malaysian customs, but one that also embraced a casual island style. Bringing together two very different cultures for a weekend-long event can be tricky, especially when your taste leans toward the nontraditional —but I love a challenge!

Adeline and Michael chose to host the wedding weekend at the Lodge at Koele, which is located some six thousand feet above sea level. Not only are there knockout views, there's a remarkable mix of weather. People from Asia (where most of Adeline's family would be coming from) tend to like the cool weather. Obviously, people from America head to Hawaii for the warm weather. Because the lodge is at a high elevation, it can get nippy, but the beach down below is generally rather tropical—a magical combo for this couple's guest list.

As we strolled the grounds of the estate during our first site visit, I started to get a better idea of what Adeline meant when she said "traditional yet different." To make this wedding a reality, I'd need to mix many of the ancient Chinese-Malaysian rituals with a casual Hawaiian feeling. I'd need to get across the couple's unique sense of humor and their elegant taste. Adeline and Michael were up for just about anything, but they definitely didn't want over-the-top floral arrangements or any other decorations that didn't blend with the landscape. By the time we finished our walk, dozens of ideas were percolating in my head. The trick would be bringing them together seamlessly.

The weekend began Thursday evening with a quick rehearsal so that everyone in the families and wedding party would know exactly where they needed to be during the ceremony. My staff and I had been rehearsing our end of the events for months, but for Michael, Adeline, and their families, this would be a first taste of what was to come. Following the rehearsal, we hosted a marvelous Asian fusion dinner for all the guests in the terrace dining room, where they could meet, relax, kick back, and reminisce about their wonderful friendships with the bride and groom.

The celebration really started to heat up the next day. At eleven-thirty A.M., a caravan of jeeps shuttled everyone from the hotel down to the beach for a fun-in-the-sun welcome party. Adeline and Michael have never been ones to sit around, and neither, it turned out, were their friends. This was an active group. They liked to hike and climb and snorkel and play volleyball. So a beach party, which would also include the many children invited, was an exhilarating way to start our wedding weekend.

The party exuded pure Hawaii. We dressed the picnic tables in grass skirts and topped them with traditional Hawaiian-print tablecloths. We covered the market umbrellas in exotic palm leaves and hanging orchids. For centerpieces, I clustered ripe tropical fruits such as pineapples, coconuts, papayas, cantaloupes, and mangos on banana leaves with blossoms of exotic orchids tucked in, giving the tables a dash of pure Carmen Miranda élan. We also brought in the best and the brightest-colored towels we could find to jazz up the chaise longues, and made sure we had a healthy supply of sunscreen on hand so guests wouldn't start the weekend with a burn. The food was everything you'd want from a beach barbecue and then some. Waiters passed out appetizers throughout the afternoon, while guests partook of our main courses, buffet style. As a starter, what about a tangy pineapple gazpacho served in a hollowed-out pineapple? What about following up with tender grilled lobster, juicy grilled prawns and langoustines, and freshly grilled salmon? And, of course, we had all

the traditional barbecue accoutrements: buttery corn on the cob, tropical cole slaw, salads, and BBQ-toasted breads. For dessert, there were apple and pecan pies, and an old-fashioned fresh-fruit cobbler.

When guests weren't enjoying the gorgeous barbecue, they were having a blast on the beach. We made sure there was plenty to keep the kids happy: rackets, pails, shovels, beach balls, and, of course, more seashells than the Little Mermaid ever dreamed of. For the grown-ups, I hired deejay Kemedji, one of the most famous deejays in Paris, to play music the entire weekend. Kemedji got the party moving and grooving with the kind of reggae that makes everybody feel fabulous.

Afterward, guests drifted back to their hotel rooms and changed for the first of the evening's activities: a sunset wine tasting on the eighteenth hole of the lodge's golf course. Michael is a great wine aficionado, and he had the incredibly chic idea of hosting a tasting to preview the wines we'd be serving throughout the weekend. The spot we picked was breath-taking (in fact, Bill Gates was married at that same spot, in 1994). We spread picnic blankets on the grass, set up wine, cheese, and bread stations, and for about an hour guests sampled Michael's eight impeccable wine selections, while the fantastic, specially flown-in sommelier, Josh Wesson, discussed each one. It was a terrific prequel to the evening's next event: a wildly elaborate Chinese dinner, which we dubbed "The Simply Red Night."

To be frank, there was nothing at all simple about this party! As Adeline and Michael's loved ones left the wine tasting, we reminded them to dress in red for dinner, which would be served at eight o'clock sharp in a specially designed Chinese pavilion–style tent near the lodge. A vaulted fabric ceiling of scarlet dupioni silk arched over walls draped in the same decadent fabric. The entire seating area was arranged on a garnet-colored carpet. The table-cloths were vermillion silk, with black seams at the corners. Guests sat on low pods covered in kumquat orange for a slight contrast, but aside from that, everyone was seeing red: The bars were ruby. We'd had the gardens surrounding the pavilion replanted with bright-red flowers. I even had lipstick-red pashmina shawls at each table, in case any of the ladies felt chilly during the evening.

The drama began before anyone even entered the pavilion. Guests strolled through a large Oriental arbor and then down a red-and-black-carpeted path toward the entrance. Trees adorned with Chinese lanterns lined either side of the walkway, and as an added touch, we'd hung fortune cookies, which contained each guest's table assignment. Once Adeline's and Michael's friends and family had plucked their table numbers from the trees, they proceeded into the pavilion through a large canopy topped by a Chinese pagoda. At the center of the pavilion sat an enormous fountain, which I'd covered almost entirely, disguising it as a four-sided banquette. Only a statue of a pineapple at the top remained showing—which played right into our Asian-island theme, not to mention that the pineapple is a symbol of friendship. Our dining area was symmetrically composed in a rectangular formation around the banquet. On either end of this dining space were two semicircular areas cordoned off by tall columns covered in black. Red silk lanterns hung from each, and we'd draped sheer black fabric between the columns to create a high-glam backdrop. The bars were housed on one side of the pavilion, with the live food stations on the other. Voilà! Suddenly the night was all about dining in the island's ultra-exclusive, sinfully luxurious Chinese restaurant. It was chic, sexy, and pure fun.

Between the courses of the dinner, a series of sparklers began hissing and exulting, and an amazing troupe of Hawaiian fire dancers appeared to perform to the beat of traditional Hawaiian drums. When they'd finished, a large gong sounded. Dinner was served! To make the meal as authentic as possible, I'd had the chefs flown in from China. The first four courses—sashimi, abalone-and-jellyfish salad, spring rolls, and honey walnut shrimp with a chiffonade of fresh mint—were plated and served tableside. But we also set woks up at sta-

tions so that people could pick and choose from curried lobster risotto, freshly prepared wok-fried noodles, and Peking duck with duck fried rice. For an over-the-top touch, we served abalone eye (actually, a fillet, or loin) finished with eighteen-carat gold leaf. After the amazing dinner, a dessert of banana beignet with vanilla ice cream and caramel sauce, lychee nuts, and, naturally, fortune cookies did the trick.

It wasn't long after dinner before everybody was ready for some action. We found ourselves pushing the tables aside so that everyone could get up and boogie. Once again, deejay Kemedji provided the tunes as master mixologist Dale DeGroff whipped up some of his one-of-a-kind cocktails. Adeline and Michael wanted spontaneity, and with this simply red evening, that's exactly what they got.

The next morning, Adeline's family hosted a brief traditional Chinese tea ceremony in the lodge's lounge. In China this is considered a sign of respect toward the groom's family. Afterward, guests lingered over tea and pastries. Then at noon, Adeline hosted a luncheon for her closest girlfriends up in her suite. All the while, my staff was busy setting up for the night's big events: the wedding ceremony, the cocktail hour, the wedding dinner, and the after-party. By six o'clock everything, and everyone, was in place.

Adeline had made it clear from the beginning that she wanted to be married in an open setting rather than indoors. One of the biggest draws of the Lodge at Koele is its expansive gardens and superlative landscape. During our first site visit, we considered setting the ceremony by a nearby waterfall, but as we strolled the grounds, we came across a cluster of enormous old trees. About one hundred yards away was a small gazebo. In my mind's eye, I began painting a picture, imagining how we could have the bride begin her walk down the aisle from that gazebo, then set the ceremony beneath these exquisite old trees. After much planning, here she was—about to take that walk to meet her soon-to-be-husband.

Of course, given the setting, there was no official aisle. Instead, I'd created a pathway made of large pieces of flagstone shipped on barges from California. We'd planted red and white flowering plants around the stone for added drama. The path meandered down the lawn to the ceremony site, which was designed in the round beneath the trees. Hanging from the trees were pod-shaped lanterns and long garlands of red, gold, and white orchids. We gave small bells to the children, who—needless to say—were thrilled to have a role to play. They rang them happily as they, the groom, and the groomsmen led guests to their seats, half of which were slipcovered in white linen for the men, and the other half in white organza for the women.

Adeline's four bridesmaids, wearing aubergine dresses and carrying spring-green orchids, led the procession. They were followed by two flower girls. The ring bearer walked with Michael. In an original, and beautifully sentimental, gesture, the ring bearer presented the ring atop the military hat of Michael's recently deceased father. Finally—as the orchestra played "Avé Maria"—the moment had come for the bride to make her way down the flagstone path. Dressed in a strapless Vera Wang gown covered in delicate lace, Adeline was glowing. The procession couldn't have been more organic in the way it fit with the magical landscape and the bride and groom's carefree personal style.

Immediately following the Maui-style wedding ceremony, two traditional Chinese lion-dancers appeared, setting off firecrackers—a tradition in many Chinese celebrations—and coaxing guests out of the chairs to form a conga line. (The lion, a symbol of power, wisdom, and good fortune, together with the firecrackers, is said to chase away evil spirits and bring happiness, longevity, and luck.)

Michael and Adeline spent a few quiet moments in the gazebo as husband and wife, while the lion-dancers led the line of guests up to the cocktail area—the same spot where we'd held the Chinese dinner the night before. But gone now was the pavilion! In its place waiters stood ready to serve champagne, Velvet Fogs (a to-die-for mix of orange-flavored vodka, fresh lime juice, Angostura bitters, Velvet Falernum liqueur, and fresh orange juice, topped with a flamed orange peel and freshly grated nutmeg), Pisco Sours (brandy, lemon juice, sugar, and egg whites), and hors d'oeuvres. The lion-dancers continued to perform until Adeline and Michael rejoined their family and friends. Now two of the guests presented a pair of red envelopes to the lions, symbolizing prosperity and happiness. The lions then danced to the nearby trees and unfurled double happiness scrolls—a traditional Chinese wedding decoration of banners with a poem written in Chinese on both sides, praising the couple and their perfect marriage. Adeline and Michael were beyond blissful.

Now we were ready for dinner. Planning an event that would rival (let alone top) the previous evening's extravaganza was a challenge, but—as I said—I'm always up for a challenge, and we managed to pull this one off with much success. Whereas our Chinese dinner had been all about red-hot theater, the reception dinner was devoted to cool, simple elegance. I'd constructed a long, narrow canopy overlooking a huge pond a short distance from the lodge. We laid an eggplant-colored rug over the dark wood floor and set up two long rectangular tables that each sat forty guests. The materials for the tables were regal but also understated— an amethyst and cream silk with an eggplant border. The amethyst linen napkins were arranged using a rectangular fold, then placed, along with the purple menu cards, atop clear-glass square plates. The centerpieces added a slight earthiness to the tables: Narrow containers, designed with purple calla lilies, purple carnations, portias, horsetails, moss, and pebbles, alternated with tall plum glass votive holders and purple glass containers filled with aubergine and green orchids, succulents, and reeds. We had the room illuminated with oversized cylindrical amethyst lanterns placed above the tables, which created a spectacularly clean, modern look. The effect was magical.

Bradley Czajka, the resident chef at the lodge, masterminded the meal, and the result was chic, refined, and mouthwatering. We began with imperial Beluga caviar served with chive

blinis, followed by Kona lobster salad wrapped in island tomatoes with morel mushrooms and basil essence. For the main course, he served fennel-dusted Hawaiian snapper on Nalo Farm greens with portabello cannelloni in a mushroom emulsion. It was beyond the beyond.

For dessert, our guests were in for a surprise. Adeline had confided to me that she wanted people to have "what they wanted" for dessert, rather than just one cake that had been chosen for them. So I came up with a solution that would offer variety yet maintain the tradition of a wedding cake. Throughout the meal, we displayed a gorgeous confection baked by legendary New York cake diva Sylvia Weinstock. However, it clearly wasn't big enough to serve all the guests. After dinner, Adeline and Michael went ahead and made the ceremonial cut when—in a moment of flawless synchronicity—out from the kitchen came countless miniature wedding cakes in all different flavors and whimsical designs, each as adorable as it was scrumptious, one for each guest. The bride was thrilled, and the guests were in ecstasy. After this amazing dessert, with charged champagne glasses, we invited everyone outside to watch a jaw-dropping display of fireworks over the pond. Everyone assumed the party was over. Everyone was wrong!

We escorted the guests back to the lodge to what had been the cocktail bar and tearoom. But I assure you, this was no tearoom anymore! We'd stripped the draperies, removed the furniture, re-carpeted the whole room in chocolate brown, and placed chocolate-brown furniture all around. We also installed an enormous dance floor. And behind the bar we placed a giant gold Buddha to oversee the festivities. The place had been transformed into an ultrasophisticated club! People danced like there was no tomorrow (including Adeline and myself), and the energy in the room was sky-high. Guests who weren't dancing were lounging and smoking cigars in the adjacent outdoor area, where they could watch a video of Michael and Adeline's trip to Africa on a giant flat-screen television. This was pure, unadulterated pleasure—the kind of night nobody ever wants to end.

But, as they say, all fun things eventually do have to come to an end. When the party was over, guests headed back to their rooms for some desperately needed sleep. There would be just one more event before Michael and Adeline called it a weekend: the next morning's tropical brunch, complete with all the elements of a proper send-off breakfast—including the requisite Bloody Marys. As Adeline and Michael ventured forth on their honeymoon, they could look back on their Lanai wedding as a dazzling blend of not only cultures and styles but friends and family.

MENU

IMPERIAL BELUGA CAVIAR

with Chive Blinis

TRIMBACH "RESERVE" PINOT GRIS 2000

∽

KONA GRILLED LOBSTER SALAD

with Island Tomatoes, Morel Mushrooms, and Basil Essence

∽

FENNEL POLLEN—DUSTED HAWAIIAN SNAPPER

on Nalo Farm Greens

PORTABELLO CANNELLONI STUFFED

with Mushroom Emulsion

WILTED GREENS AND RED BEET EMULSION

OLIVIER LEFLAIVE "PERRIERES" MEURSAULT 1999

∽

MEA'ONO

(Pineapple Cookies)

MINIATURE WEDDING CAKES

VEUVE CLICQUOT DEMI-SEC NV

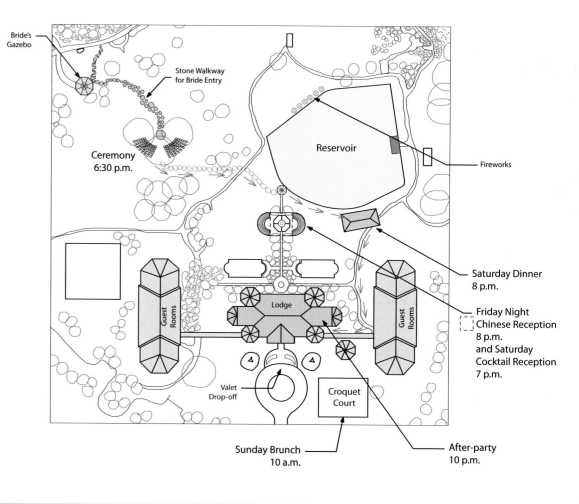

YOURS, MINE, AND THEIRS

Some brides and grooms want their weddings to be held in a child-free zone. Others find that inviting kids—of both family and friends—only enhances the festivities. Whether you're planning a weekend-long destination wedding or a more low-key affair, here are some thoughts on choosing a location that'll make both parents and kids happy.

Make it clear well in advance which events are kid friendly and which ones aren't.

Arrange for baby-sitters, which many hotels provide. If you know how many children will be attending, go the extra mile to reserve enough sitters ahead of time (of course, always check in with the parents). At Adeline and Michael's wedding, for example, we arranged for group baby-sitting in one of the hotel's conference rooms during the adults-only events. We stocked the area with two televisions, plenty of DVDs, games, popcorn, and blankets.

Find fun ways to involve the children in the ceremony. Busy children are well-behaved children. If you assign them a task, they'll usually perform it with gusto, which can add to the festive atmosphere. The children at Adeline and Michael's wedding had a blast ringing the bells as they led guests to their seats.

If you're hosting children at the reception itself, have the chef create a special children's menu. Consider having children older than five sit at their own supervised table. The children at Adeline and Michael's wedding didn't attend the reception dinner, but they still had to eat. So in the conference room we'd set up, the chef prepared a dinner of hot dogs, chicken nuggets, and French fries.

Have a list of family-friendly activities available for the downtime between wedding events. Nothing is worse for parents—and children—than to be cooped up in a hotel room trying to figure out where to go and how to get there. Enlist the help of the hotel's concierge to do this.

GARDEN OF EARTHLY DELIGHTS

Andrea Reisman and Matt Johnson

ASPEN, COLORADO

JUNE 9, 2001

Some

couples want their wedding to be white tie and tails, pomp and circumstance—and I'm happy to provide all of the finger bowls and top hats their hearts desire. But Andrea Reisman and Matt Johnson had something a little different in mind. They wanted wildflowers and bonfires, picnics, games, and long hikes in the bracingly fresh Colorado mountain air. They wanted their wedding to be a summer camp for grown-ups.

Andrea and Matt had been to Aspen in the winter, but they'd never experienced its lush majesty on a summer day. One look at how the mountains and valleys turn emerald green, the rivers run high, and the fields overflow with a profusion of delphinium, larkspur, daisies, and sunflowers, and these two nature lovers were completely hooked. There was yet another selling point: Their friends and family were coming from Canada, the East Coast, and the West Coast, so Aspen was a major plus geographically.

With Mother Nature as our inspiration, we decided to create an enchanted secret garden. Every detail of the event would celebrate our wondrous Rocky Mountain surroundings. The linens were done in cornflower blues and pistachio greens; curly willows and mosses wound their way through the floral arrangements; our welcome brochures were adorned with twigs and beautiful pressed flowers; and dried leaves garnished the dinner menus.

Our first task? To find a space that would accommodate 250 people. We quickly realized the easiest solution was to build one ourselves. Two enormous canopy tents would house the ceremony, the dinner, and later (with an expertly timed quick changeover of the ceremony room, while guests were still feasting), the after-party. The renowned Little Nell Hotel, tucked into the base of Aspen Mountain, would serve as our hub, our hive, and our heaven. Their chefs would do the catering, and many of Matt and Andrea's guests would stay at the resort for the weekend.

The festivities began on Friday morning, with early-arrival guests paddling down roaring rapids on an exhilarating white-water rafting trip. After catching their breath and toweling off, they enjoyed lunch at the Aspen Club, high atop Ajax Mountain, with panoramic views of the towering pines and snow-capped peaks.

Friday night's welcome dinner was the first "official" get-together of the weekend: an authentic country cookout deep in the heart of Castle Creek at the Elk Mountain Lodge. My team set up redwood benches and tables by the pond and illuminated the place with tiki torches and lanterns so everyone could see the deliciously green valley below. The picnic tables were accented with red-and-white gingham napkins and dotted with jam jars brimming over with field flowers to ensure an authentic country setting. We also scattered plush blankets on the lawn, as well as portable heaters, to ward off the chill of the Colorado nighttime air.

As a country-and-Western band rocked and smoke poured from the lodge chimney, guests dug into a hearty all-American buffet: grilled chicken, homemade buttermilk biscuits, hamburgers, hot dogs, steak, and delicious corn on the cob. It was impossible to feel anything but energized and utterly, casually at ease. Guests arrived in jeans and sweatshirts, and even those who'd met only a few hours earlier laughed together as if they'd been friends for decades. When the evening came to a close, a few of us took places around a billowing campfire, roasting S'mores, while others hunkered inside the lodge, playing Who Wants to Be a Millionaire? (Naturally, all questions and answers related to Andrea and Matt, and family members delighted in sharing stories about the bride and groom.)

All day Saturday, guests were left to explore the glorious surrounding areas. But at dusk, just as the sky turned a magnificent mother-of-pearl hue, it was time for the moment we'd all been waiting for. Friends and family members made their way through a pair of six-foottall wrought-iron gates to the entrance of the ceremony tent. The gates themselves were an exquisite sight, completely blanketed with roses, ivies, passion vines, and sinuous willows, giving guests just a hint of what awaited them inside.

When the second, inner gates opened—to the delicate strings of harps playing—our Eden was revealed, and after a brief, awestruck moment of silence, the *ooohs* and *ahhhs* began.

No one could believe what they were seeing: The sides of the tents were lined with dozens

of leafy green trees. Shrubbery and blooms sprouted up all around us as we took our places in a semicircle, beneath a pale-ginger canopy ceiling that had all the luscious drama of a gigantic Georgia O' Keeffe blossom. Through the tent's wall of windows, we could look out at the spectacular mountains looming in the distance. Although we were sheltered, it felt as though we were still outdoors.

At the center of the tent, we'd constructed a gazebo, covered with a rich tangle of vines, leaves, and thousands of Virginia, Polo, Iceberg, and Sahara roses. The look was wild and unkempt, as if this mystical garden had been there for hundreds of years, undiscovered and untouched and, until now, unimagined. The bridesmaids wore two styles of dresses, both designed by Richard Tyler, one silver, the other icy blue, while Andrea was a breathtaking vision of simple elegance in a strapless Pamela Dennis A-line silk gown with a crystal-beaded bodice and hem.

After a simple, beautiful ceremony, the champagne flowed and the good times rolled. Waiters passed appetizers: spring vegetable risotto in espresso cups and tuna tartare and caviar, both served on spoons. Then, with their cocktails finished and spirits soaring, guests were ushered into the two-tiered dinner canopy. Here, they discovered the main floor, arranged as a formal, classical garden, straight out of Versailles: a twenty-seven-foot-high ceiling draped in filmy shades of soft mountain sage, fawn, vanilla, and ginger; cascading fountains; a pair of shimmering wishing ponds; and stunning candelabra centerpieces topped with rose and hydrangea topiaries. The six twelve-foot-long tables were dressed in cornflower-blue and pistachio-green silk taffeta, and overlaid with a glistening organza in the same palette. Our stemware was a moody mix of deep aubergine and chartreuse green, as were the matching votive candles along the length of the table.

The second tier, a wraparound elevated seating area, looked every bit as intoxicating. We'd concocted a forest of fairy-tale proportions by framing both the walls and ceiling with a lattice intricately woven with vines and greenery. Dangling from the ceiling, like grape clusters spilling from their vines, were thousands of Dendrobium orchids and candles. The centerpieces for the tables on this tier were metal trees with branches reaching to the ceiling, as if anchoring our opulent arbor.

While everyone was marveling at this magical, mystical space, another extraordinary transformation was quietly taking place in the ceremony tent. There, a large staff was lifting up the carpets and stage, removing the walls and the gazebo, and installing a flat ceiling. In a

mere one and a half hours, our ceremony in-the-round had become a chic urban nightclub, complete with ruby-red lighting, a Mondrian-inspired dance floor, a sleek zebra-patterned lounge, and several sexy patent-leather bars.

Following a delicious dinner of breaded veal chops and crisp garlic-and-shallot potatoes—and a series of heartfelt toasts to the jubilant bride and groom—Andrea and Matt rose to cut the cake, a Polly Schoonmaker original that fit beautifully into our garden theme. Polly had hand-sculpted and hand-painted marzipan berries, buds, even honeybees, and sprinkled them over all four tiers of cake, incorporating a classic country lattice pattern into the icing.

When guests returned to what was now the after-party tent, they entered through a curtain of jet-black beads to discover a black mirrored bar serving up an assortment of exotic martinis and over-the-top sinful desserts. Once everyone was revved into full party mode, legendary Paris deejay Claude Challe spun into action, serenading guests with the Doors' "Light My Fire" as we unveiled our final surprise of the evening: We had lit the entire mountainside—visible through the back windows of the tent—a vibrant shade of red, and fired up pots of golden dancing flames in the surrounding fields with a projected image of the bride's and groom's initials.

But it wasn't just the guests who were surprised: A few inquisitive black bears were spotted meandering down from the mountains. Either they were serious fans of Jim Morrison, or they, too, wanted to see what all the ecstasy was about. We served a light breakfast at around one A.M., but unfortunately had to unplug Claude when the Aspen police paid us a polite cease-and-desist visit at three A.M. On Sunday morning, the festivities carried on with a farewell brunch before our guests finally departed Aspen, filled with memories for a lifetime.

MENU

BELUGA CAVIAR,
Served on a Spoon

∾

FRESH FROM THE SEA
Medallions of Lobster, Oysters, Alaskan King Crab, Jumbo Prawns,
Mussels, and Clams on the Half Shell with Cocktail Sauce
(served family-style)

∾

BREADED VEAL CHOP
with Arugula, Tomato, and Basil Salad

CRISP GARLIC-AND-SHALLOT POTATOES

TOASTED HEAD CABERNET SAUVIGNON SYRAH 1998

∾

WEDDING CAKE

ASSORTED DESSERTS

DOM PÉRIGNON 1993

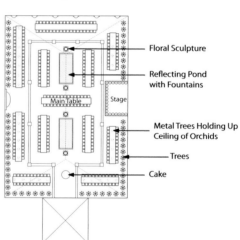

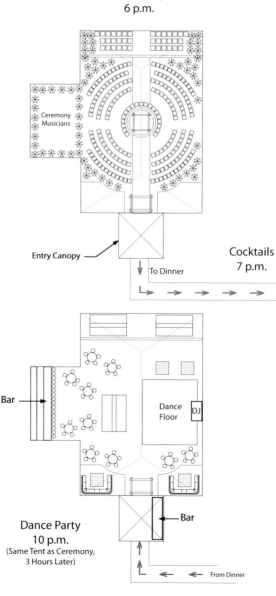

Ceremony
6 p.m.

Ceremony Musicians

Entry Canopy

To Dinner

Cocktails
7 p.m.

Dinner
8 p.m.

Floral Sculpture

Reflecting Pond
with Fountains

Main Table

Stage

Metal Trees Holding Up
Ceiling of Orchids

Trees

Cake

Bar

Dance Floor

DJ

Bar

Dance Party
10 p.m.
(Same Tent as Ceremony,
3 Hours Later)

From Dinner

THANKS FOR THE MEMORIES

Guest ledgers are often fifty-page books, but as they enter, family members and friends usually scribble their names on the first three pages without much forethought. What's so special about an autograph, and, more important, what are the bride and groom supposed to *do* with it?

A fresh approach to this tradition is to pass around memory books at dinner—or if your wedding celebration is an entire weekend, over the course of several days. In Andrea and Matt's case, we requested that guests fill the pages with wonderful stories and personal notes that the newlyweds could reread and treasure for the rest of their lives.

The book you choose can be as simple as a blank journal you pick up at your stationery store and cover in a fabric that corresponds to the wedding motif, or as intricate as an album you've collaged with beautiful photos. One of my favorite rituals is to give each guest couple a yard or so of thick ribbon and a magic marker to write wishes on. They can do this during the reception, or beforehand, in their hotel rooms, and then bring it with them to the ceremony. These wishes are all suspended from the arbor, or the area under which the bride and groom marries, with the couple then taking their vows under the collective good wishes of their family and friends. After the ceremony, the ribbons are all rolled up, placed in a decorative box, and presented to the newlyweds.

Give guests a few suggestions regarding what they might like to write: a meaningful anecdote about the bride or groom (or both); a touching story that explains why these two individuals are so unique and adored; a poem or song lyric that captures the spirit of the day; even a favorite moment from the wedding. As the book or card gets passed from hand to hand over dinner, friends can share these memories with the rest of the table.

Finally, tie your books with a gorgeous piece of ribbon, or seal them in a box or envelope for the bride and groom to open on their first anniversary. Though it's tempting for them to sneak a peek at what everyone has written, the surprise will be well worth the wait.

MEXICO BY MOONLIGHT

Sarah Siegel and Gary Magness

COSTA CAREYES, MEXICO

October 20, 2001

*I*nspiration comes in many forms. A movie you've loved since childhood, a bracing walk in the January snow, anything by Mozart or Tina Turner—that's all a given. But I've also been known to find inspiration in a theme song from a James Bond movie, in the colors of a display of Granny Smith apples, in a restaurant that offers a delicious delicacy, or even in a simple scrap of fabric.

There was nothing simple about the exquisite swatch of French brocade that inspired Sarah Siegel and Gary Magness's wedding. Reminiscent of ancient Aztec art, it was a vibrant mosaic of persimmon, scarlet, magenta, and emerald green laced with real gold thread, and for Sarah—whose strong affinity for color and design has brought her terrific success in the fashion industry—and me, it was love at first sight.

Sarah asked that I find an exotic location, so off to Mexico I went. I found heaven in Costa Careyes on Mexico's Pacific Coast, and suggested that we set the wedding there. It's sexy, exotic, and less than a four-hour flight from Denver, where the couple live. Nestled in the hillside around a sapphire-blue bay, this chic enclave is made up of forty-two houses done in a contemporary Mexican style by architect Louis Barragàn, every one in a different vivid color: shocking pink, saffron yellow, azure blue. To gild the lily just a bit more, these one-of-a-kind homes mingle with bougainvillea that grows as far as the eye can see in lush profusions of fuchsia, tangerine, and gold. The result is a mind-boggling explosion of color. And for this one special weekend, we secured some of the most spectacular homes Careyes has to offer for Sarah and Gary's guests.

My mission was to weave the wedding around a single patch of this Aztec-style brocade, so with my fabric sample in hand, off I went to scour the crowded streets and markets from Guadalajara to Mexico City (and all points in between), searching for just the right unifying elements. In my mind's eye, I imagined a long banquet table dressed in all the brilliant jewel-tones found in my small sample of fabric. The table would be set with glass and pottery crafted by local artisans, inside a *palapa* (thatch hut) situated on a grassy lawn next to the sea, bordered by pearl-white sand, lapping waves, and the magnificent Mexican moonlight.

A confession: Before I really came to know Mexico, I considered the food to be somewhat pedestrian. From what I could gather, it was a none-too-subtle mix of rice and beans, chips and guacamole. I couldn't have been more wrong. When I first met Juan Andrea Romero, one of the most innovative chefs in Mexico City, I told him I was looking for authentic home cooking, and asked that he prepare some of his grandmother's favorite recipes for me. He responded by completely reeducating me about the art of Mexican cuisine. Each and every dish was complex, delicate, fragrant, and utterly unlike anything I'd ever tasted before. Just remembering that fantastic meal makes me want to jump on the next plane.

Señor Romero's food would delight us all weekend, starting with a Friday-night welcome dinner at the fabulous Casa Sol de Oriente; followed by a Saturday-afternoon picnic in paradise; culminating in an out-of-this-world wedding feast; and concluding with a farewell brunch on Sunday. Designer Ellen Weldon included all these details in a tri-fold invitation, which she then wrapped in the same beautiful signature brocade fabric and hand-tied with a green-and-gold ribbon.

On Friday morning, fifty-eight of Gary and Sarah's dearest friends, family members, and a customs agent (who would check passports during the flight to save guests from headaches upon arrival) boarded a chartered 737 from Denver to Manzanillo, a sleepy coastal resort and the site of the nearest airport. Once on the plane, we began the celebration with (what else!) margaritas, and a screening of the magical Mexican romance *Like Water for Chocolate*. It was an ideal way to set the mood for all that lay ahead. Guests were greeted on the tarmac by a trio of guitarists, then whisked away in cars stocked with icy Mexican beer, soda, tea, and chilled lavender-scented hand towels.

After the luxury of a chartered flight, a seamless trip from the airport, and the downtime of a siesta, guests were well rested, relaxed, and absolutely over the moon to be there. Of course, they only felt more settled when they found a charming, handcrafted little tote bag waiting for them, filled with everything a traveler could possibly need. Far too often, a destination wedding like this one starts off on the wrong foot thanks to tedious travel— multi-legged flights, an arduous trip once the plane lands, and guests being jostled from the airport directly to the rehearsal dinner, late and exhausted. The weekend rarely recovers from this harried start. Not so for our party.

After refreshing themselves, it was on to the magnificent Casa Sol de Oriente for a sunset soiree and another chance for guests to get acquainted before the wedding. The palette for

the party, of course, had to be sun-inspired—*Sol de Oriente* means "sun of the Orient." The large *palapa*-influenced house is surrounded by an infinity-style swimming pool that wraps itself 270 degrees around all sides. To play off the house's bright-orange exterior, the tables were draped in simple handcrafted ripe papaya-colored cloths overlaid with orange and yellow sunburst silk, set with alternating yellow and orange Mexican-crafted charger plates. Amber votives surrounded vases bursting with orange and yellow zinnias and marigolds. Playful, welcoming, fabulously light-drenched—this was a dinner that created brand-new friendships and enriched great old ones.

Guests stood on the patio overlooking the pool, drinking in the vastness of the Pacific (along with margaritas, strawberry and mango daiquiris, sangria, and mojitos), listening to the raucous music of a mariachi band. Dinner was served on the top balcony in casual buffet style: butterflied shrimp in a garlic-chile sauce; fresh smoked marlin; corn-cake quiche; white snapper tamales; salad of grilled cactus leaf, cilantro, tomato, and onion; and, of course, an irresistible assortment of *dulces,* or Mexican sweets.

The next morning, after a hearty breakfast of *huevos rancheros* (eggs scrambled with Mexican chorizo and peppers) and fresh-squeezed guava nectar, guests were free to relax at the pool or participate in some of the incredible activities Careyes offers—everything from a nature hike to canoeing, scuba diving, deep-sea fishing, horseback riding, and golf. At noon, small fishing boats took everyone on an enchanting coastline tour to a picnic at the private Playa Paraiso, a secluded cove where hundreds of palm trees surround sky-blue waters and immaculate white sand.

As the boats pulled into the cove, waiters were standing thigh-high in the water, holding trays of blended margaritas and frosty Mexican beers. As protection against the harsh Mexican sun, we constructed star-shaped canopies of white canvas, trimmed in cream leather and staked into the ground on bamboo poles. Underneath, navy and white deck chairs, fluffy white towels, and zinc buckets (dug in the sand, and spilling over with ice-cold beer) set a scene of pure comfort and indulgence. How often do we get to experience the taste of perfectly fresh seafood? Because there's truly nothing better, lunch was a sumptuous seafood barbecue of grilled spiny-tailed lobster, giant prawns, and gorgeous, gleaming fish caught earlier in the day and cooked over a huge open fire. Afterward, some guests chose to swim off their lunch and play ball, while others napped beneath the palms. No one wanted to leave our hideaway . . . but it was time to prepare for the evening's festivities.

At eight, all the guests, many of whom were strangers to one another a mere twenty-four hours before, congregated on the hotel patio, now bonded in friendship. Spiritual adviser Dr. Linda Garbett, my friend of many years, acted as officiant, calling the group to order by ringing Tibetan bells seven times. The procession, accompanied by strumming Mexican guitarists, wound through the lovely *casitas* (small houses) and down a tiki-torch-lined path to an elegantly dressed *palapa* on the nearby beach known as Playa Rosa.

Our ceremony took place at the water's edge between two enormous palms. As a focal point, and for an added helping of drama, I created a backdrop with more than one thousand crystals dangling on monofilament forming the shape of a six-foot-high cross. The full moon shone through the crystals, and they gently chimed in the balmy breeze as an accent to the soft strumming of the classical guitars. The effect was mystical and mesmerizing.

On the arm of her proud father, Mo Siegel, the bride glided down the aisle—a carpet of Gerber daisy heads graduating in color from white at the top of the aisle to magenta at the foot, woven along the grass. Her two-year-old daughter, Camryn, made an angelic flower girl. Sarah's gown by Richard Tyler had a delicate mermaid look. It was crafted of layers of shredded tulle in the colors of the sea, and beaded with Swarovski crystals that shimmered in the light. In her hair, she wore tiny gilded starfish.

Linda spoke of Sarah's and Gary's love as only she can, while guests listened, enraptured. Now the couple exchanged their vows and embraced beneath the glowing moon. We cheered the new Mr. and Mrs. Magness with flutes of champagne poured from magnums of Dom Pérignon 1990, accompanied by mini *empanadas* and *taquitos.*

Now it was time for the party to move to an adjacent *palapa* for dinner.

The dinner table was dressed in a rich emerald-green dupioni silk undercloth, then topped with our rich and colorful Aztec brocade French fabric, hemmed with a thirty-inch macramé fringe in rich green that skimmed the ground. The chairs were also covered in an emerald-green, tight-fitting dupioni silk cover, then strapped with bustiers around their backs, also fashioned from the brocade. On the table was a trio of assorted vase styles, some in gold leaf, some in gold mosaic, some in green mosaic, all brimming over with lush Gloriosa lilies and tropical orchids. After quite a hunt, I'd discovered a fantastic Italian plate with a gold-leaf floral pattern sandblasted onto the surface, and had the remarkable local artisans in Guadalajara create beautiful clear-glass dishes to place on top. Emerald-green glasses, also handcrafted by local artisans, and napkins in the same emerald-green silk trimmed with a gold rickrack, unified the palette. Finally, we'd scattered dozens of votive candles in gold glass holders down the table, and a celestial glow suffused the ceiling from seventy-five different-sized three-dimensional metal Mexican stars.

Dinner began with a stuffed chipotle pepper with rice and meat, drizzled with a walnut-and-pomegranate-seed sauce, followed by a refreshing salad of local greens and mango, and a tower of Baja lobsters and prawns. The main course was a filet of beef with a trio of moles—the wonderfully complex sauces that contain as many as three dozen ingredients (typically including chocolate!)—followed by a superb warm chocolate truffle with macadamia-nut ice cream. Amidst the celebration, there was also a somber moment of remembrance: Sarah acknowledged that the wedding was just a little over a month after the tragedy of September 11. She spoke from the heart about how truly fortunate she and Gary felt to be able to share this time with the friends and family who meant so much to them.

The cake-cutting took place under yet another *palapa.* Polly Schoonmaker and I had designed a four-layer masterpiece of carrot cake with cream cheese–mascarpone filling. We replicated the motifs of the Aztec fabric used on the dining table, taking hours to stencil and apply the elaborate pattern. The cake was iced with buttercream, enrobed with tangerine-and-deep-persimmon-colored fondant, and bejeweled with gold leaf. At the top, rather than the traditional bride and groom, we placed a starburst of sugared gems.

At the very moment Sarah and Gary cut the first slice, fireworks erupted outside, creating a breathtaking pyrotechnic curtain of starlight. The traditional Mexican fireworks display lasted ten minutes while ten large pyres were simultaneously lit on the beach. *Spectacular!* is an understatement. The after-party had everyone dancing to disco music supplied by the beyond-fabulous Parisian deejay Kemedji. Finally—at nearly two in the morning and after a light breakfast—guests returned to their villas to find on their pillows a slip of paper with a wish written on it, and a bottle of premium tequila, a souvenir of our amazing fiesta.

Sunday morning yielded a very special close to the weekend. The word *careyes* means "tortoiseshell," so we decided—rather impulsively—that a turtle blessing was called for. There is a turtle reserve on one of the beaches at Careyes, and we collected sixty baby turtles (one for each guest), and asked the guests to make a wish for the newlyweds, then release the tiny creatures into the sea. It was a truly extraordinary end to a truly extraordinary weekend.

MENU

CHILE ANCHO EN NOGADO (STUFFED CHIPOTLE PEPPER)

with Rice and Meat, with a Fresh Walnut and Pomegranate-Seed Sauce

JERMANN "WERE DREAMS" FRIULI 1999

∾

ENSALADA VERDE CON MANGO Y ADEREZO DE GUAYABA
Y TORRE DE CAMARONES Y LONGOSTA

*(Salad of Greens and Mango Tossed in a Guava Dressing Presented
with a Tower of Baja Lobsters and Prawns)*

∾

FILETE DE RES EN MANTEQUILLA DE TRES MOLES

(Filet of Beef with a Trio of Moles)

PAPA SOUFFLÉ

(Potato Soufflé)

CESTITO DE VEGETALES

(Pasta Basket of Fresh Steamed Vegetable Sticks)

SAN VINCENTE RIOJA 1998

∾

TRUFA EN TIBIO DE CHOCOLATE Y NIEVE DE MACADAMIA

(Warm Chocolate Truffle with Macadamia-Nut Ice Cream)

POSTRE DE VODA

(Wedding Cake)

DOM PÉRIGNON 1996

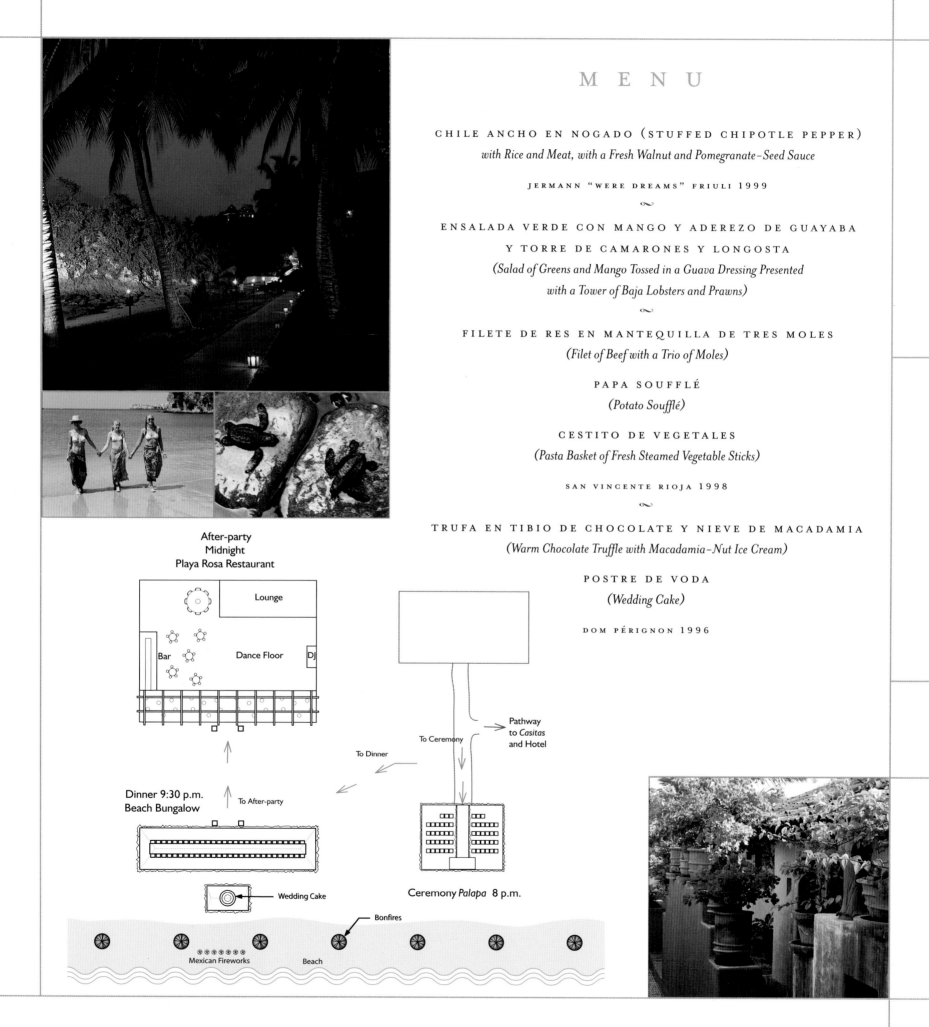

After-party
Midnight
Playa Rosa Restaurant

Lounge

Bar

Dance Floor

DJ

Dinner 9:30 p.m.
Beach Bungalow

To After-party

To Dinner

To Ceremony

Pathway
to *Casitas*
and Hotel

Wedding Cake

Ceremony *Palapa* 8 p.m.

Bonfires

Mexican Fireworks

Beach

YOUR PLEDGE OF ALLEGIANCE

There's no rule that insists your vows have to be the standard "Do you take this woman/man to be your lawfully wedded wife/husband?" Instead of the boilerplate "till death do us part," your vows are your chance to be powerful, personal, even poignant, voicing why you fell in love and what makes your relationship so meaningful. They can evoke the beauty of your surroundings and even the collective spiritual energy of your guests. Linda Garbett wrote these beautiful vows for Sarah and Gary. Perhaps you can draw inspiration from them when writing your own, or give them to your officiant as an example to follow:

"We are gathered in the name of love at sunset by the water's edge in this magnificent cathedral of nature to celebrate the marriage and the intertwining destinies of Sarah Siegel and Gary Don Magness, who, through being wonderfully, bravely, and truthfully themselves, have fallen in love and chosen to be married. So come now. Open your hearts and turn off your minds. We've come together to celebrate and have fun, to see what magic and moonlight have done, to see how love can make a king and queen of a man and woman. We're here to listen, to love, to laugh and cry. To sing, dance, and rejoice and to send them into their future with one gigantic blessing.

"Gary, do you now choose Sarah to be your wife? To share your life openly with her, to accept her fully as she is, and delight in who she is becoming? To respect her uniqueness, encourage her fulfillment, and compassionately support her through all your years together?"

"I do."

"Sarah, do you now choose Gary to be your husband? To share your life openly with him, to accept him fully as he is, and delight in who he is becoming? To respect his uniqueness, encourage his fulfillment, and compassionately support him through all of your years together?"

"I do."

"As God is a circle whose center is everywhere, and whose circumference is nowhere, so let the seamless circle of these rings become the symbol of your endless love. May the light of God shine on the passageways to your dreams. May you know the sweetness and the power of a promise kept for a lifetime."

ACKNOWLEDGMENTS

This book has been a dream in the making and has taken many years to bring to fruition. I am most grateful first and foremost to all the couples who entrusted me to design and orchestrate the most magical day of their lives. Thank you for your inspiration, laughter, and trust. Most of all, thank you for the wonderful friendships that have endured.

The weddings in this book would never have taken place without the hard work and support of my incredibly dedicated and professional staff, who have traveled around the world with me, creating "fabulous" for our brides and grooms. Thank you to the producers: Jodi Cohen, Laine Sutten, Hillary Gutstein, and all our CCL staff who've assisted me along the way. And to my business partner David Berke for your guidance and expertise on every single project, directing us onto the right path and keeping us out of trouble!

There are countless people around the globe who have worked and collaborated with us on flowers, décor, lighting, sound, staging, logistics, transportation, hair, and makeup; not to mention all of the musicians, deejays, chefs, sommeliers, hotel managers, valets, and executive assistants. Without your assistance, this dream of mine would never have been possible. You have all played, and continue to play, a very important role in the success of Colin Cowie Lifestyle. I thank you all from the bottom of my heart. You were the ones who did the heavy lifting, and without you, none of these weddings would have come alive the way they did.

This book would never have been possible were it not for the amazing images captured by our talented photographers: Julie Skarratt, Joe Buissink, Deborah Finegold, Stephanie Jasper and Paul Sky, Mallory Sampson, Robert Isacson, Robin Layton, Elliot Holtzman, and Garett Holden—thank you for capturing such wonderful memories for us. Thank you to photographer and photo editor Colin Miller, for all your hard work and passion that is so clear in these images.

My voice in this book sounds just like me because of my collaboration with two of the most wonderful, gifted, and talented writers I have ever had the privilege and pleasure to work with. Thank you, Lisa Kogan and Peter Smith—it was a blessed journey. My editor at Clarkson Potter, Aliza Fogelson, and art director Marysarah Quinn and designer Jennifer Beal—thank you for the passion and guidance you brought to this project. My agent, Margret McBride, who has been with me from day one, thank you for believing in me and my vision.

As always, I thank my mother, Gloria Cowie, who instilled in me vast doses of passion, and taught me to believe that anything is possible. I am eternally grateful for these gifts and for your love.

And finally, I thank my soul mate and business partner, Stuart Brownstein, for your extraordinary support and passion, both in life and in business.

COLIN COWIE's renowned parties have made him a favorite of Oprah Winfrey, Jerry Seinfeld, John Travolta, heads of state and royalty, and many others—and secured his place as one of the most sought-after wedding planners in the world. He appears regularly on *The Oprah Winfrey Show* and *The Early Show* and is a frequent contributor to *O Magazine*, *Brides*, and *People*. Born in Zambia and raised in South Africa, he now resides in New York. Colin Cowie Lifestyle, his event-planning, interior-design, and lifestyle company, is based in Los Angeles and New York. Please visit him online at www.colincowie.com.